A Balm in Gilead Eulogies of Comfort

Compiled by Randall C. Webber

BK Royston Publishing | 502-802-5385
http://bkroystonpublishing.com

© Copyright – 2019

All Rights Reserved. No part of this book may be reproduced, stored in a retrieval system, or transmitted by any means without the written permission of the author.

Cover Photo of Image: Dr. Randall C. Webber
Cover Layout: Elite Cover Designs
Back Cover Photo Credit: Dujuanya Renee Johnson

Eulogy for the Young Victims of the Sixteenth Street Baptist Church Bombing: Typescript is reprinted by arrangement with the Heirs to the Estate of Martin Luther King Jr., c/o Writers House as agent for the proprietor, New York, NY. Copyright © Dr. Martin Luther King, Jr. © renewed 1992 Coretta Scott King.

Eulogy for the Honorable Reverend Clementa Pinckney is presented, courtesy of the National Archives and Records Administration's Barack Obama Presidential Library.

Scripture taken from the NEW AMERICAN STANDARD BIBLE®, copyright © 1960, 1962, 1963, 1968, 1971, 1972, 1973, 1975, 1977, 1995 by the Lockman Foundation. Used by permission.

THE HOLY BIBLE, NEW INTERNATIONAL VERSION® NIV® Copyright © 1973, 1978, 1984 by International Bible Society®. Used by permission. All rights reserved worldwide.

Cover art: *Jacob's Ladder*. Sandra Charles. ©2019. Used by permission.

ISBN-13: 978-1-946111-95-1

LCCN: 2019916852

Printed in the United States of America

Preface

Death strikes down all humans. Each person's life progresses inexorably toward a mortal conclusion to which nobody is immune. One individual may die during infancy, or even be stillborn, while another's lifespan might encompass an entire century. One may die suddenly, tragically, unexpectedly, or violently, and another after suffering for a long time with an agonizing illness. One's death circumstance might create a stigma in the perceptions of the survivors, while another's might seem glorious or at least honorable. One might be laid to rest with much pomp and circumstance and another receive a pauper's burial with few in attendance. As Martin Luther King, Jr. noted, death is a most democratic experience.

Death is an ever-present reality in all congregations. At any time, at least one parishioner is dying, recently deceased, or coping with bereavement. Consequently, a minister must be prepared to serve the grieving at any time, in accordance with the culture of the bereft. Equally importantly, the minister must serve the bereft in accordance with his or her Christian identity.

This volume examines African American funerals through the lens of the funeral sermon or eulogy. In each case the eulogizer wrestles with tension occasioned by the status of death both as an irrevocable separation from the living and as a portal to the deity's presence.

As a Caucasian editor, I am entirely unable to invent an African American eulogy. Consequently, I am grateful for my contributors' offerings. Without those genuine African American funeral sermons, this volume would have been impossible to create. Two federal libraries were of great assistance. I am grateful for the courtesy extended by the National Archives and Records Administration's Barack Obama Presidential Library regarding my presentation of Obama's eulogy. The Library of Congress facilitated the presentation of Pompey's eulogy and also made available the entire collection of Federal Writers' Project materials and all three volumes of Newton and Cowper's *Olney Hymns*. Furthermore, I am grateful to the heirs to the estate of Martin Luther King, Jr., c/o Writers House as agent for the proprietor, New York, NY, for the privilege of publishing, possibly for the first time, the previously obscure typescript of the *Eulogy for the Young Victims of the Sixteenth Street Baptist Church Bombing*.

Three other libraries also provided assistance and materials for this volume. Bellarmine University's William Lee Lyons Brown Library provided access to multiple copies

PREFACE v

of Charles Ball's narrative. Louisville Presbyterian Theological Seminary's Ernest Miller White Library allowed me to use numerous materials from their Black Church Studies collection. Southern Baptist Theological Seminary's James Petigrew Boyce Centennial Library facilitated the procurement of resources relating to early Christian practices. All of these repositories made important contributions to the completion of the volume.

The libraries' contributions notwithstanding, this volume focuses on the contributions of African American clergy and public speakers called upon to provide comfort by situating specific deaths within the larger contexts of African American culture and Christian hope. To each, I extend my heartfelt appreciation.

Winston Bennett is embarking on a new career as a motivational speaker after experiencing some setbacks as a basketball coach. He is an alumnus of the University of Kentucky's basketball program and one of two contributors who is not a minister.

George and Shirley Burke have a long tenure as co-pastors of Coke Memorial United Methodist Church in Louisville's Smoketown neighborhood.

Robert O'Keefe Hassell is a young evangelist who trained as an educator (M.Ed., Ed.D.) and accepted his call to the ministry reluctantly. He is the founder of Sinai Evangelistic Ministries, Inc. and is active in Kingdom Love Worship Center, Church of God in Christ, Madison, TN.

Gerald J. Joiner is senior pastor of Zion Baptist Church, Inc. in Louisville's Russell neighborhood. He has a background not only in ministry but also in sales personnel management and in missions.

Martin Luther King, Jr. served as pastor of Dexter Avenue Baptist Church, Montgomery, AL (1954-1960), and as co-pastor of Ebenezer Baptist Church, Atlanta, GA (1960-1968). He is noted for his use of non-violent, direct action, modeled on that of Mahatma Ghandi, to advocate for full civil rights for African Americans. He received the Nobel Peace Prize in 1964. Like the individuals he eulogized, he was assassinated.

In her role as a chaplain for Sentara Hospice, Hampton, VA, Nicole Danielle McDonald ministers to patients with terminal illnesses and their families. She is a D.Min. alumna of Louisville Presbyterian Theological Seminary and a Ph.D. candidate in African American preaching and sacred rhetoric at Christian Theological Seminary, Indianapolis, IN.

Barack Hussein Obama, II, like Bennett, is not a member of the clergy. During a career as a community organizer, he received a J.D. from the Harvard University Law School. He subsequently became an Illinois state legislator, achieved national prominence as an orator, and served his state as a U.S. senator. His career culminated with a pair of terms as the 44th president of the United States (2009-2017).

Pompey was an emancipated slave of the Gaillard family of Winnsboro, SC. Though he apparently had no formal education, he seems to have been influenced by the worship style of Saint John Episcopal Church, his former owners' congregation, and by emerging patterns of African American and Caucasian hymnody.

Next, I wish to thank all who provided logistical support for the project. Dr. Brooke B. Webber proofread several chapters. Pelham Lyles and her staff at the Fairfield County (SC) Museum facilitated research pertaining to the Dixon/Walker narrative. The staff of Highland Baptist Church, Louisville, KY, allowed me to photograph the windows in their fellowship hall. Dr. Wade Kotter of Weber State University sent scans of a text from *Zion Songster*. Sandra Charles provided the beautiful cover painting. Dujuanya Johnson took the back cover portrait. Alamy Stock Photo provided images from Birmingham, AL and Charleston, SC. Finally, Julia Royston, my publisher, gave unflagging support and constructive criticism throughout the composition and publication process.

The Unity Monument at Louisville's Sheppard Square housing project was designed by Zephra Mae Miller and installed by her uncle, noted sculptor Ed Hamilton. This memorial served as the focal point of the book's final, brief meditation.

CONTENTS

Preface iii

The Partial Acculturation of
American Funerary Practice 1
    RANDALL C. WEBBER

Can You See Yourself Being There One Day? 39
    WINSTON GEORGE BENNETT, III

A Blessed Man 47
    GEORGE AND SHIRLEY BURKE

A Culminating Conversation! 53
    ROBERT O'KEEFE HASSELL

A Mighty Man of Valor:
Eulogy for Taurean Delon Joiner 65
    GERALD J. JOINER

Eulogy for the Young Victims of the
Sixteenth Street Baptist Church Bombing:
Typescript 79
    MARTIN LUTHER KING, JR.

In Remembrance: Saying Good-bye
and Honoring a Legacy 93
    NICOLE DANIELLE MCDONALD

Eulogy for the Honorable
Reverend Clementa Pinckney 111
  BARACK HUSSEIN OBAMA, II

The Dying Thief: Eulogy for Wash Moore 131
  POMPEY

Smoketown Get-Down Welcome Remarks 151
  RANDALL C. WEBBER

Works Cited 157

Early Sources 163

General index 167

1

The Partial Acculturation of American Funerary Practice

RANDALL C. WEBBER
WAYSIDE CHRISTIAN MISSION
LOUISVILLE, KY

     Consider a hypothetical Protestant funeral. On the night before the service, the decedent's remains are placed in a casket, typically surrounded by flower arrangements. The casket may be open or closed, depending on the family's preferences. Relatives and friends stand beside the casket as other acquaintances file through to express their condolences. Most visitors stay at the funeral home briefly, then continue with their evening responsibilities. This ritual typically is called a viewing, visitation, or wake.

     The funeral service normally occurs the morning after the viewing. Depending on the extent of the family's religious activity, the service may take place at the funeral home or at a church. Frequently, the decedent's life story and death circumstance create a tension between solemnity and celebration during the service. In my Baptist tradition, the service typically culminates with a sermon or eulogy. Other Protestant traditions may place more emphasis on their counterparts of the Lord's Supper. The length of the service varies with the family's religious orientation.

Immediately after the service, the funeralgoers form a procession, usually vehicular, to carry the remains to the cemetery. During a brief service, the minister commits the remains to the earth and the deceased into the hands of a merciful God. When the decedent is a servicemember or veteran, additional rituals specific to the military culture may be included. After the benediction, the mourners depart as cemetery personnel cover the vault and fill the grave. Eventually, a headstone may be installed over the grave, and the family and friends may commemorate the decedent's life by adorning the grave with flowers and other tokens of remembrance. In addition, one or more spontaneous memorials may be erected at sites associated with the decedent's life or death.

I have officiated funerals for both African American and Caucasian decedents and have attended many funerals officiated by other ministers. Almost all of these worship services have occurred more or less in the manner of the hypothetical funeral described above. The general contours of the Protestant funeral are evident across denominational, generational, racial, and other boundaries.

Nevertheless, with respect to certain characteristics, African American and Caucasian funerary practices exhibit some differences. The following list is representative rather than exhaustive. A Caucasian viewing, visitation, or wake is likely to be somber more often than not. At an African American ritual of this sort, in contrast, displays of emotion are more commonplace. Funerals among both races are likely to begin with a processional. In most Caucasian churches, the casket is rolled down the center aisle to the front of the sanctuary, to be met by the officiating clergy. In African American funerals, the casket is likely to be at the front of the sanctuary already, and the clergy and/or the decedent's relatives proceed down the center aisle to their places. Most Caucasian preachers remain solemn in the ways that they communicate the Christian hope in the unavoidable presence of death. Many African American preachers, in contrast, will begin in a quiet, somber manner but build up to a livelier, more festive conclusion. Audience response during sermons is nonexistent in some Caucasian churches and limited in others. In many African American funerals, in contrast, audience participation gives the eulogy an almost dialogical quality. Grave decoration for both races focuses on flowers for all decedents and on flags for servicemembers and veterans. African Americans, however, are more likely to add other objects important to the decedent or otherwise of sentimental value.

African Americans and Caucasian Americans have been living in some proximity and learning from each other since the early seventeenth century. Most of the Europeans were familiar with Christian traditions, and some Africans who were brought to the Americas as slaves had been exposed to Christian or Islamic practices in their native lands. Furthermore, humanity's 100% mortality rate has created a universal necessity of sanitary corpse disposal and rituals to help the survivors manage their loss and perpetuate the social order, even as a society's individual constituents change by means of birth, death, and other transitions. It is no surprise, then, that African American and Caucasian traditions have mingled and acculturated to shape American Protestant funerary practices.

At least three religious trends have contributed to the development of funerary practices during the past few centuries. First, the religious and spiritual practices of the tribes from which many slaves were taken have contributed to the practical aspects of ritual practice around the time of death. In fact, these tribes' traditions have provided imagery which has reinforced and gradually been merged into similar biblical imagery. Second, the Second Great Awakening placed a premium on individual experience and audience participation in religious observances. Third, the more settled liturgy of the traditional churches provided a structure and numerous worship aids for services. We now survey these three influences briefly.

African Traditions

A large proportion of the slaves brought to the Americas came from the west coast of the Angola-Congo region in central Africa.[1] Thus BaKongo traditions are especially relevant to the development of American cultural practices by the slaves and their Caucasian owners and associates. The cosmogony of these tribes postulated the existence of the following two worlds: This world in which we exist, and the other world of spirits. The other world, separated from this world by water, provided a life free of difficulty and injustice for the assorted ancestors, ghosts, witches, and other spirits who resided there.[2] The lack of difficulty and injustice, in turn, led to the conclusion that death was a loss for the survivors but a "homegoing" for the decedent.[3] The ways in which this belief system might differ from and those in which it might be compatible with a Christian doctrine of the general resurrection and afterlife are readily apparent. In fact, I have attended a number of funerals, some Caucasian but a majority African American, which were labeled "homegoing" services.

The understanding of death as a "homegoing" to a realm free of misery found a ready audience among slaves

---

[1] Suzanne E. Smith, *To serve the living: Funeral directors and the African American way of death* (Cambridge/London: Harvard Univ., 2010), 20.

[2] *To serve the living*, 20-21.

[3] *Ibid.*, 18.

subjected to extreme difficulties. During the 1830's, a book purportedly by Charles Ball, noted the presence of a large number of slaves from Africa in the South Carolina low country during Ball's time there (c. 1804-1806) and implied that this situation no longer prevailed during the 1830's. Ball characterized the Africans' religious practices pejoratively as ones based on witchcraft, conjuration, and the agency of evil spirits, likely an external perspective regarding the status of various beings in the other world, according to BaKongo cosmogony.[4] Given the location, it is probable that the traditions Ball described represent an early stage in the development of Gullah/Geechee culture.

Ball described the death of an infant, followed only a few months later by his mother's death. The authenticity of Ball's book has been questioned; some have suggested that it was written by Caucasian abolitionists. However, authenticity is not pertinent to our evaluation since the book evidently met the tests of plausibility and verisimilitude when it was published. Moreover, the transcriber proved entirely incapable of achieving his stated objective of recording the facts in a simple narrative while minimizing subjective statements. Thus, the transcriber's ability to invent facts is doubtful at best. In other words, the book, whether or not factually correct, provides an accurate

---

[4] *Slavery in the United States: A narrative of the life and adventures of Charles Ball, a black man* (Lewiston, PA: John W. Shugert, 1836), 126-127.

description of the behaviors prevalent in situations such as those narrated.

The burials occurred in the vicinity of Charleston between 1804 and 1806, about thirty years before the book was published. A slave named Lydia had symptoms that we would associate with pulmonary tuberculosis. When Lydia's infant died shortly before Christmas, Ball assisted her and her husband with the burial. The husband had been a priest in his native religion before he was brought from Africa to South Carolina. He buried some tribal objects with the infant in order to help his kinfolk recognize the infant when he should return to Africa. Ball summarized Lydia's sentiments as follows:

> As we returned home, Lydia told me she was rejoiced that her child was dead, and out of a world in which slavery and wretchedness must have been its only portion. "I am now," said she, "ready to follow my child, and the sooner I go, the better for me."[5]

Lydia's wish was granted the following March. She died of "consumption of the lungs" (i.e., pulmonary tuberculosis), and Ball buried her remains beside those of her infant and closed the grave. Ball's assessment, after the fact, was that "death was to her a welcome messenger, who came

---

[5]*Slavery in the United States*, 205.

to remove her from toil that she could not support, and from misery that she could not sustain."[6]

Spirituals that substantiate the prevalence of Lydia's perspective among African American slaves are abundant. *Deep river*, *Oh freedom*, and *Soon I will be done with the troubles of the world*, for example, reflect a Christianized perspective but remain compatible with the traditional BaKongo orientation. In each case, the spiritual used the metaphor of rest/relief or that of crossing a body of water as a double entendre to describe both death and freedom.

Likewise, some hymns from European Protestant traditions, circulating widely in hymnals from the southern states, characterized death as relief from earthly toil or used the image of the Israelites crossing the Jordan River as a metaphor for the passage from mortal life through death to the resurrection. Martin Luther's *Mit Fried und Freud ich fahr dahin* fits into the first category and Isaac Watts' *There is a land of pure delight* and Samuel Stennett's *Promised land*, explicitly a commentary on Watts' text, into the second. The first category, of course, was compatible with Lydia's conception of death and the second with the BaKongo traditions of water as both a barrier and a passageway between the two worlds. These hymns, like the spirituals, had much in common with the imagery inherent in many indigenous traditions.

In a practical sense, African funerary practices had their greatest impact by creating an American tradition of elaborate funerals and grave decorations that surmounted

---

[6]*Slavery in the United States*, 206.

racial divisions. If a funeral were a "homegoing," it should be a celebration of the decedent's release from earthly toil. This rationale was not uniquely African American. Luther expressed the opinion concisely: *"Wie Gott mir verheissen hat, der Tod ist mein Schlaf worden."*[7]

The custom of sparing no expense to honor the deceased with a first-rate funeral and headstone is well documented. This practice is no more racially unique than is the presence of celebration in some funerals. The Bethel AME Zion and Concord Presbyterian Churches, each of which has a cemetery, are located about a mile apart in Fairfield County, SC. The Bethel cemetery holds the remains of Ned Walker, who described Pompey's eulogy (pp. 131-150), his wife, two daughters, and the Walkers' grandson. The Concord cemetery holds the remains of a number of locally prominent individuals, including members of the Brice family, possibly related to the Walt Brice of the narrative. A cursory examination of the size and quality of the headstones and the general condition of the cemeteries indicates that the Caucasians who buried their relatives in the Concord cemetery went to at least as much effort and expense to provide memorials as did the African Americans who used the Bethel cemetery. The Caucasians presumably had more money to spend on such memorials. The fact that

---

[7]More idiomatically than grammatically: "As God has assured me, death will become my repose." Mit Fried und Freud ich fahr dahin, in Johann Walter, *Ein geystliche Gesangk Buchleyn* (Wittenberg, 1524).

they chose to spend their money in that manner indicates that they shared African American neighbors' interest in elaborate funerals. The cost of such funerals and burials frequently was high enough to create dilemmas for the survivors. As burial insurance purveyor Robert A. Cole explained, "For some of our policyholders, their Metropolitan funeral was, sadly enough, the biggest, most impressive event of their lives."[8]

The commemoration of the deceased did not cease with the erection of a headstone. Grave decoration remains a shared African American and Caucasian tradition. The use of flags to decorate servicemembers' and veterans' graves and of flowers more generally crosses ethnic and racial divisions. In addition, BaKongo grave decoration customs are not extinct among African Americans. Some graves may be decorated with empty bottles and broken jars, pots, and household items to represent the decedent's transition to the other world (BaKongo) or into Jesus' presence (Christianized).

A sidewalk memorial to a deceased, African American resident of Louisville, KY: This memorial, erected in 2019, features not only a cross but also some flower arrangements, three bottles (one uncapped), and a broken brick. The cross, of course, is a Christian symbol; the flowers represent a cross-cultural practice; and the other items are reminiscent of traditional BaKongo grave decorations.

[8]*To serve the living*, 102. Cole founded Chicago's Metropolitan Funeral System Association to provide burial insurance and managed that company for many years.

The hymnic repertoire for antebellum funerals, like grave decoration preferences, has a cross cultural aspect. As noted above, both spirituals and hymns might reflect BaKongo and Christian beliefs that were compatible. However, an anthology of excerpts from the Federal Writers' Project's ex-slave interviews indicates that the three hymns most remembered from antebellum-era funerals did not follow that pattern. One interviewee recalled *Why do we mourn departing friends* by Isaac Watts; two remembered *And am I born to die* by Charles Wesley; and three mentioned *Hark from the tombs* by Watts.[9] While these texts reflect a Christian understanding of death and resurrection, they bear little similarity to BaKongo doctrines regarding the same topics.

These former slaves' recollections also are explicit regarding the influence of Caucasian owners and clergy on funerary practices. In fact, three of the four informants indicated the master's involvement in funeral preparations or the use of Caucasian clergy to preach the funerals. In one case, the master, a minister, officiated and eulogized the deceased slave. Moreover, the hymns noted above were popularized in Caucasian publications. *Sacred Harp* and *Southern Harmony*, the most prevalent fasola hymnals of the late antebellum period, included all three hymns. Of course, the slave narratives are products of their geographic

---

[9]*Memories of the enslaved: Voices from the slave narratives*, ed. Spencer R. Crew, Lonnie G. Bunch, III, and Clement A. Price (Santa Barbara/Denver: Praeger, 2015), 27-29.

provenance. Three of the four informants resided in Georgia, as did Charles Wesley during the eighteenth and the *Sacred Harp* compilers during the nineteenth centuries.

A closer examination of a narrative that mentions two of these hymns provides a clearer picture of the role of Caucasians in a former slave's religious experience. Jefferson Franklin Henry recalled that his relatives attended the Baptist churches to which their owner and some of the owner's relatives belonged and that Caucasians attended the slave funerals at which the hymns were sung.[10] He noted also that slaves were not permitted to become literate. For that reason, he identified the hymns as cultural artifacts that had not been committed to writing but were handed down verbally. His assessment, of course, was inaccurate for those particular hymns but might provide a reliable indication of the ways culture could be transmitted in a society with limited levels of literacy.

Henry's account notes similarities between slave and Caucasian funerary practice. Coffins, for example, were built the same way, the only difference being that the ones for Caucasians were stained. Other sources indicate that both races had customs regarding the wake. Hamp Kennedy of Mississippi recalled that "at de wake we clapped our han's an' kep' time wid our feet—Walking Egypt, dey calls hit—an' we chant an' hum all night 'till de nigger was

---

[10]"Jefferson Franklin Henry," Federal Writers' Project, *Slave narrative project*, vol. 4, Georgia, part 2, Garey-Jones, 185-187. Washington DC: United States Works Projects Administration Records, Manuscript Division, Library of Congress, 1941.

funeralized."[11] In light of his comments, it is possible that the text of *Oh freedom* provided a metaphorical depiction of a slave's wake. Charles Ball described a wake for a Caucasian abduction victim who died of her injuries. Ball's master hosted the event at his house, providing the guests with desserts, fruits, and wines as they visited and stayed briefly to pay their respects to the bereaved.[12] After a long procession and a short funeral, the master provided a repast for about one hundred of the funeralgoers, another cross cultural tradition.

The former slaves' recollections of funerals and Ball's account of an upper class, Caucasian wake and funeral provide examples of mutual acculturation, with owners and slaves learning from each other's funerary practices that they found compatible. Another example of acculturation is evident as well. Many descriptions from both races note that a corpse might be bathed prior to the wake and burial. The early appearance of this primarily Islamic practice in the southern states is explained by Ball's realization after the fact that some slaves whom he met in the South Carolina low country were Muslims.[13]

---

[11]"Hamp Kennedy," Federal Writers' Project, *Slave narrative project*, vol. 9, Mississippi, Allen-Young, 86. Washington DC: United States Works Projects Administration Records, Manuscript Division, Library of Congress, 1941.

[12]*Slavery in the United States*, 199-200.

[13]*Ibid.*, 127.

So far, we have examined funerary practices from an Afrocentric perspective. This inquiry has demonstrated that some aspects of traditional BaKongo cosmogony and some dimensions of Caucasian Christian metaphor were compatible, and others more distinctive. At this point, we describe some influential Caucasian practices.

Caucasian Worship Styles

During the antebellum period, Caucasians expressed their religious sentiments through a variety of worship styles. Within the possibilities created and limits imposed by their technology, their liturgies might take a number of forms that we might consider exuberant and spontaneous, on the one hand, or formal and controlled, on the other.

This variety of worship styles is evident throughout the colonial era. Among Baptists in the southern states, for example, Sandy Creek (NC) Church was noted for its spontaneity and Charleston First (SC) for its formality as early as the mid eighteenth century. In fact, the Charleston congregation retained a high level of formality long after its founders, migrants from Maine, passed from the scene.

Nevertheless, differences in worship style are most evident in materials from the revivals of the first third of the nineteenth century. It is not much of an exaggeration to say that those forms of worship prevalent in frontier areas during the Second Great Awakening emphasized exuberance, spontaneity, and emotion. Among the large camp meeting crowds, some individuals might have emotional outbursts, exhibit strange behaviors, or even be "slain" (collapse).

These behaviors, then, might be seen as manifestations of the Holy Spirit and thus as evidence of Christian conversion. This worship style would receive renewed emphasis in the twentieth century Pentecostal movements, both African American and Caucasian.

The subsequent New England revivals provided a different orientation. The clergy in that region generally considered outward (emotional) signs of conviction at most evidence that those displaying such signs recognized their need for religion. This recognition stopped short of the regeneration that was the ultimate goal of conversion. For these clergy, the continuation and ultimate fruition of the conversion process depended on the continued intervention of the Holy Spirit. This process, they believed, occurred silently, sometimes so silently that the occurrence or lack thereof of conversion was not immediately evident.[14] Thus the New England revivalists exhibited a more cognitive approach, sometimes to the point of removing congregants from the service if they were to become too emotionally demonstrative. Lyman Beecher, for example, recalled that his friend Asahel Nettleton preached sermons which were highly intellectual, doctrinal, and decidedly Calvinistic.[15]

Three nineteenth century hymn texts illustrate the different worship styles prevalent during the nineteenth

---

[14] Iain, H. Murray, *Revival and revivalism: The making and marring of American evangelicalism, 1750-1858* (Edinburgh/Carlisle: Banner of Truth Trust, 1994), 210.

[15] *Ibid.*, 199.

century. *Brethren, we have met together* was written in 1819 by George Atkins, a Methodist preacher active in Ohio and Tennessee. This text casts an exuberant camp meeting, with the congregation participating actively, in a positive light:

> Brethren, we have met to worship,
> And adore the Lord, our God.
> Will you pray with all your power,
> While we try to preach the word?
> All is vain, unless the spirit
> Of the Holy One come down;
> Brethren, pray, and holy manna
> Will be shower'd all around.
>
> Sisters, will you join and help us?
> Moses' sisters aided him;
> Will you help the trembling mourners,
> Who are struggling hard with sin?
> Tell them all about the savior,
> Tell them that he will be found;
> Sisters, pray, and holy manna,
> Will be shower'd all around.[16]

Another hymn from the frontier illustrates both the importance and the possible drawbacks of an emphasis on the emotional aspects of worship. A verse of *See how the scriptures are fulfilling*, an 1807 text by John Adam Granade, a Methodist preacher active in North Carolina and

---

[16]As in William Walker, *Southern harmony and musical companion* (Philadelphia: Miller & Burlock, 1854), 103.

Tennessee, takes the form of a debate between proponents and detractors of an exuberant worship style.

> Ten thousand fall before Jehovah
> For mercy—mercy! loud they cry.
> They rise, all shouting, "Hallelujah!"
> And "Glory be to God on high:"
> But others cry, "It's all disorder,"
> And disbelieve God's holy word;
> Yet Christians sing and shout the louder,
> "All glory, glory to the Lord."[17]

Hymns also illustrate the intellectual approach more prevalent in New England. One might be challenged to describe the deity's silent work in poetic format. Phillips Brooks, an Episcopal priest who had been a child in Boston during the latter years of the revival period, accomplished this task by turning his attention to the more concrete doctrine of the incarnation. The visual basis of the poetry, his view of Bethlehem after dark, is quite well attested. The philosophical foundation, the characterization of the deity's redemptive work as a silent, barely noticeable process, has received less attention:

> How silently, how silently
> The wond'rous gift is giv'n.

---

[17]As in Peter D. Myers, *Zion songster: A collection of hymns and spiritual songs, generally sung at camp and prayer meetings, and in revivals of religion*, 3rd ed. (New York: J. S. Redfield, 1850), 129.

So God imparts to human hearts
The blessings of his heav'n.
No ear may hear his coming,
Yet in this world of sin,
Where meek souls will receive him still,
The dear Christ enters in.[18]

Contemporary Practices: A Partial Acculturation

At this point we may resume our consideration of the hypothetical, Protestant funeral service. However, we will specify that the service is representative of those held in African American churches. The service is labeled a "homegoing," even if the decedent died prematurely and tragically. It occurs during the mid to late morning hours the day after the wake. Depending on the circumstances, there may be an additional opportunity for visitors to express their sympathy immediately before the funeral. Either burial or the removal of the corpse for cremation follows the service immediately. In the event of burial, the more typical arrangement, a procession from the church to the cemetery is followed by a brief commitment service. The event concludes with the decedent's family and friends holding a repast, a dinner which may be quasi-ceremonial but also gives the participants a chance to unwind after the day's events.

As the service begins, female attendants, usually attired in white uniforms, are stationed near the back of the sanctuary. These personnel are called nurses, owing to the

---

[18]Hymn text: O little town of Bethlehem, v. 3, as in *Sursum corda* (Philadelphia: American Baptist Publication Society, 1898), 121.

similarity of their uniforms to those worn by nurses during an earlier era. These attendants assist worshippers who may become emotionally expressive to the extent that they disrupt the service. Such assistance usually occurs in the sanctuary but, in extreme cases, may include the removal of those overcome until they regain sufficient composure to rejoin the service.

The funeral begins with a processional. Relatives of the decedent process to their seating area. Participating clergy process to their places on the stage, either before or after the family processes to their seats. Frequently, the minister leading the clergy processional will recite Psalm 23 as he or she walks up the center aisle.

Beginning with the invocation, the service generally follows an order of worship. In most cases, a bulletin distributed to worshippers at the entrances to the sanctuary enables all to be aware of the order in which events will unfold. The order of worship varies with denominational customs and the family's preferences. However, remarks by participating clergy and musical selections are common components. The highlight of the service, at least in those denominations that emphasize proclamation rather than the Lord's Supper, is the eulogy. In most cases, the decedent's pastor or a minister who is a relative or friend delivers the eulogy. This sermon frequently starts in a somber, low-key manner and builds up to a lively, celebrative conclusion. It normally is longer than most Caucasian funeral sermons.

This typical description illustrates the presence of African American traditions, Caucasian styles conducive to emotional expression, and Caucasian practices that depend more heavily on formality. The "homegoing" terminology, with its BaKongo roots, the opening processional, and the eulogy are modeled on antebellum African American customs, some shared or compatible with contemporaneous Caucasian practices. Of course, Caucasian funerals have their own processionals, usually moving the casket rather than the family and/or clergy. Those denominations that emphasize proclamation use the eulogy as the service's culminating event, but the sermon usually is shorter and more subdued than its African American counterpart.

The nurses play a role similar to that of the sisters at the camp meeting, as described in *Brethren we have met together*. Their role encompasses two different functions. On the one hand, the nurses encourage those prone to emotional displays to show their emotions. They assure the mourners that such displays are normal responses to an abnormal situation. On the other hand, the nurses preserve the decorum of the service by intervening and guiding the mourners gently before their emotional displays become so pronounced as to disrupt the service.

The use of an order of worship, disseminated to all by means of a bulletin, has its roots in the more formal practices of the liturgical churches. This practice keeps the service on a predictable path toward completion. The emotional expression inherent in a bereavement situation takes place within the boundaries articulated by the order of worship.

I found out about the extent to which some African American worshippers value the formal order of worship in a most surprising way. At one funeral in which I had a minor role, things came to a sudden, unexpected pause early in the service. The minister sitting next to me nudged me and asked me to get things under control, which I did by announcing the next speaker's name and organizational affiliation. I was surprised that he asked me to take care of the issue. I was not officiating, and this other minister could have known only that I was a Caucasian colleague. Actually, I had helped the next-of-kin prepare the bulletin while the pastor was unavailable and then reviewed it with the pastor when he returned, so I was thoroughly familiar with the way the service was meant to proceed. In this case, my brief prompt was sufficient to get the service back on track.

African American funerals, in short, draw from a variety of traditions. During the antebellum period, African Americans and Caucasians lived and worked in proximity to each other. This proximity included participation in worship. Each group taught and learned from the other; the former slaves' reports agree on these points. Nevertheless, funerary practices have not evolved into a monolithic amalgam. African American and Caucasian funerals have combined many of the same elements into distinct worship styles, each of which provides comfort and hope.

The Partial Acculturation of Bereavement Theory

BaKongo cosmogony presumes that death separates an individual from the living incompletely. A deceased individual who carried out the ancestors' orders and tried to assure the welfare of the clan would be admitted to Mpemba, a blessed world of the ancestors without the various tribulations afflicting this world. Conversely, a life characterized by selfish behavior might destine a decedent to become a wandering spirit.[19] These various spiritual beings, in turn, might return either to instruct or to curse the living. Consequently, the BaKongo postulated the presence of both beneficent and malevolent behavior by the dead toward the living. The fourth gospel's emphasis on the intervention of the Paraclete, a surrogate for the absent Jesus, represents an inexact parallel from the Christian scriptural corpus.

In its early days, classical bereavement theory shared one presumption with BaKongo cosmogony but subscribed to the opposite of the other postulate. On the one hand, both traditions acknowledged the separation of the living and the dead. On the other hand, psychoanalytic theory initially characterized the separation as complete and irrevocable. The lack of any particular concept of the afterlife in psychological writings reflects that discipline's inherent empiricism, that is, to its self-limitation to the study of observable phenomena. Inherent in that lack, however, is the presumption that whatever may occur after death is an

---

[19]Simon Bockie, *Death and the invisible powers: The world of Kongo belief* (Bloomington/Indianapolis: Indiana Univ., 1993), 83-84.

external issue, not amenable to direct observation by the living.

Death's Cold, Sullen Stream:
Classical Conceptualizations of Bereavement

An early essay by Sigmund Freud represents the first systematic consideration of bereavement from a psychoanalytical perspective.[20] In this work, Freud noted the pervasiveness of symptoms frequently associated with major depression (melancholia) and characterized the symptoms as byproducts of a situational crisis likely to run its course with little intervention.[21] Mourning eventually enables an individual to sever his/her ties to the lost object. In Freud's tripartite conceptualization, such ties are broken with difficulty since they reside primarily in the libidinal functions of the mind, but the ego (the more rational part) eventually comes to terms with reality and frees the person from his/her ties to an object that no longer exists.

An informative evaluation of Freud's thought must take into account the circumstances in which Freud wrote the essay. World War I was raging in Europe in 1915, so Freud probably had exposure to a number of young war widows. In such cases, the elimination of psychological ties to the deceased husband, followed eventually by their replacement

---

[20]Mourning and melancholia, *The standard edition of the complete psychological works of Sigmund Freud*, tr. James Strachey (London: Hogarth/Institute of Psycho-Analysis, 1957 [1915 orig.]), 14:243-258.

[21]*Ibid.*, 243-244.

with similar ties through remarriage, might constitute a rational objective of the process.

During the next 50 years, Freud's thought served as a springboard for the further examination of bereavement. Erich Lindemann further elaborated Freud's descriptions of depressive symptoms as he related his experience treating patients bereft suddenly by the 1942 Cocoanut Grove fire.[22] In 1964, Elisabeth Kübler-Ross interviewed terminally ill patients regarding their experiences. On the basis of these interviews, she postulated a theory of stages by which those experiencing anticipatory grief might progress from the initial shock of their diagnoses to acceptance of their conditions and inevitable fates.[23]

Freud's conceptualization of mourning as progress toward the severance and replacement of ties with the deceased remained an unquestioned presumption until the last decades of the twentieth century. However, buried in Freud's essay was a hint that separation might be only a part of the process. While mourning represented progress toward the eventual replacement of old libidinal ties with new ones, the process could prolong the existence of the lost object at least in the psyche of the bereft individual.[24] This possibility

---

[22] Symptomatology and management of acute grief, *American journal of psychiatry*, 101/2 (Sept., 1944), 141-148.

[23] *On death and dying: What the dying have to teach doctors, nurses, clergy, and their own families* (New York/Toronto: Macmillan, 1964).

[24] Mourning and melancholia, 245.

aligns bereavement theory more closely to the traditional BaKongo concept of partial separation.

Blest Be the Tie That Binds:
Louisa Gaillard and Ned Walker

On April 1, 1902, a former plantation owner named Louisa Gaillard died in Winnsboro, SC. Her death became a news item not only in Winnsboro but also in Columbia, where she had been active in Daughters of the American Revolution. Neither her age nor her socioeconomic status precipitated this public interest. The obituary in the *State*, still Columbia's primary newspaper, emphasized her hereditary status as the daughter of an officer who served with Francis Marion.[25] For the inhabitants of Columbia in 1902, Louisa Gaillard's death marked the removal of one of the last direct links to the Revolutionary generation. After her death, Columbia's residents needed to redefine their ties to the Revolutionary generation and, through those ties, their own identities as patriotic Americans. The presence of the Civil War as a living memory gave this redefinition a special urgency for residents of the capital of the first state to secede and initiate military action.

About 35 years after Louisa Gaillard's death, Ned Walker, a former Gaillard slave, recalled a conversation he

---

[25]Death of Mrs. Louisa Gaillard: Was born in 1809 and was daughter of a Revolutionary officer, The *State*, April 5, 1902, p. 6, col 4.

had with Louisa Gaillard during the Reconstruction era.[26] In that conversation, Louisa Gaillard asked Ned Walker not to consider her and her deceased husband his "old" (former) mistress and master. Walker agreed to remember her admonition and implied that the conversation was his reason for choosing intentionally to continue addressing Caucasians with the formal titles Marse (Mr.) and Miss. Moreover, Walker envisioned Gaillard in heaven singing the Episcopal hymns ("chants") that, in his opinion, she sang beautifully in her church in Winnsboro. Walker was elderly by the time he was interviewed; public documents provide various dates of birth between 1849 and c. 1860.

Ned Walker's self-reported behavior indicates that he and his former owner chose not to sever but to maintain and redefine their relationship. Walker's preference for the formal address formerly prescribed as a form of deference enabled him to establish his place in the post-war social order and to continue associating with the Caucasians who had been part of his pre-war life. Moreover, his assumption that Louisa Gaillard was in heaven praising God indicates that he had both a positive regard for her and a hope for eventual reunification in the afterlife. In any case, more than seventy years after emancipation, he maintained sufficient contact with the Gaillard family to inform his interviewer that one of Louisa and David Gaillard's sons had moved to the state's coastal region and had died about two years before the interview.

---

[26]William Dixon's edited transcript of his interview with Ned Walker is presented in this volume (pp. 131-150).

The Gaillard family and their former slaves began redefining their relationship shortly after the thirteenth amendment freed the slaves. Walker reported that Louisa Gaillard's son Henry gave the former slaves new names and helped them register as residents in their own right. Furthermore, Henry Gaillard arranged for the former slaves to buy much of his family's Spring Vale plantation in a seller-financed transaction so they could live together on the farmland they had worked as slaves. For their part, the former slaves established their own African Methodist Episcopal congregation to preserve the polity ("form") they experienced in the owner's church while striking out in their own direction regarding hymnody and worship style ("substance"). The former slaves further memorialized their connection to the Gaillard family and the plantation by naming their church Springvale.

Will the Circle Be Unbroken?
Bereavement as Redefinition

The behavior of the Gaillard family and their former slaves after emancipation illustrates an understanding of adaptation and its most extreme example, bereavement, that theoretical literature would describe many years after Ned Walker's and Louisa Gaillard's children died. Freud had suggested in his 1915 article that the existence of a lost love object could be prolonged, at least in the psyche of the bereft. This suggestion was a minor point; its elaboration awaited attention from a later generation of bereavement theoreticians. Toward the end of the twentieth century, a number of practitioners and theoreticians turned their attention to this point. In their thought, helping a client modify and redefine, rather than sever, his/her ties to the decedent was a legitimate objective of therapy. Therese Rando's hybrid model of the grief process, incorporating both a stage theory and a functional approach, exemplifies this conceptualization.[27] In Rando's model, grief facilitates the accomplishment of the following tasks by the bereft:

Phase 1: Avoidance
   Recognize the loss,
Phase 2: Confrontation
   React to the separation,
   Recollect and re-experience the deceased and the relationship,
   Relinquish the old attachments to the deceased and the old assumptive world,
Phase 3: Accommodation
   Readjust to move adaptively into the new world without forgetting the old,
   Reinvest.

The theoretical emphasis on redefining rather than severing ties to the deceased may seem abstract. This line of thought, however, becomes more concrete as it takes shape in a sermon. Two eulogies in this volume exemplify the

---

[27]*Treatment of complicated mourning* (Champaign, IL: Research Press, 1993), 45.

focus on redefining ties and preserving connections. Winston Bennett spotlights his status as a carrier of the life lessons learned from his father, arguing that even his imperfections contribute to the consolidation of his father's legacy. Nicole McDonald advocates redefinition most directly with her focus on rituals of remembrance and use of a sermonic text predicated on two such rituals, Passover and the Lord's Supper.

In many cases, the repeated telling of stories about their experiences with a decedent helps the bereft ascribe meaning to their losses and determine the ways they will redefine and perpetuate the decedent's legacy. Since this tendency is inherent in the cognitive and emotional processing of object loss, narrative approaches may prove beneficial in helping the bereaved cope with difficult circumstances. The Federal Writers' Project's interviews of former slaves, conducted during a period of economic hardship (1936-1938), may be seen in such a light. More importantly, a eulogy creates an early opportunity to place the decedent's life in a larger perspective and to suggest possible continuations of that life story. In the current volume, this tendency presents itself most clearly in the typescript by Martin Luther King, Jr. In this eulogy, the author expressed the hope that the murder of four children in a Baptist church and the assassinations of civil rights activists elsewhere might lead to the renewal of direct, non-violent action and eventually to racial reconciliation and equality. More than fifty years later, Barack Obama characterized the object of his eulogy as an heir to the activist traditions of his church and advocated the continuation of such activism on both the political and the personal levels.

In summary, death creates a cognitive dissonance in the experience of the bereaved. On the one hand, death creates an easily observed separation which is irrevocable in the current life. On the other hand, death facilitates the redefinition of ties between the bereaved and the decedent. The first dimension has received considerable attention in the theoretical literature of the professional bereavement community. Various forms of the second dimension derive from different cultural traditions. Christianity, Islam, and some forms of Judaism subscribe to doctrines of an afterlife including possible reunification. BaKongo spirituality also has a concept of the continued existence and intervention of the deceased. Acknowledgement of separation, coupled with encouragement to redefine ties to the deceased, even to the point of distorting the character of those ties, constitutes a mutual but partial acculturation of the monotheistic and BaKongo concepts of such relationships. Consequently, an effective eulogy holds the separation of the living from the dead and the continuation of relationships in a creative tension. We now turn our attention to this paradox.

The Eulogy in Rhetorical Perspective

Rhetoric addresses the questions of who/to whom, what, where, when, and why regarding a spoken or written artifact. A funeral sermon fits into the classical rhetorical typology as an epideictic (ceremonial) oration, perhaps with deliberative components. Within this rhetorical type, the eulogy is a praise/blame speech. However, the preacher is not trying to make a case of the sort an attorney might attempt to establish in a forensic setting. Consequently, the eulogy may focus beneficially on the positive aspects of the decedent's legacy. Acknowledgement of the negative aspects helps to ensure basic honesty and believability, but an overemphasis on the pejorative creates the risk that the larger perspective might turn in an unintended direction.

Pompey's eulogy (131-150) epitomizes a healthy balance of praise and blame. The sermon acknowledges the decedent's status as a convicted larcenist explicitly but moves quickly to a description of the good he did in his job as a blacksmith. The eulogy concludes with a verbal depiction of the decedent reaching the top rung of Jacob's ladder and entering heaven.

Winston Bennett, George and Shirley Burke, Gerald Joiner, Nicole McDonald, and Barack Obama situated their eulogies clearly in the epideictic tradition of praise. The sermons by McDonald, Joiner, and the Burkes tended toward deductive and those by Bennett and Obama toward inductive reasoning. Nevertheless, all five emphasized the positive accomplishments of those whom the sermons memorialized.

The circumstances of some deaths might create a risk of retaliatory violence. In such situations, a funeral sermon takes on particular urgency as a means to reframe tragedy and direct the listeners toward more ethical, uplifting responses. The typescript version of the eulogy for the

Sixteenth Street Baptist Church bombing victims (79-92) falls into this category, as does *I have a dream*, its secular precursor. As some civil rights activists began to question the adequacy of direct, non-violent action, King included substantial deliberative components in both speeches to advocate non-violence as the most appropriate response to domestic terrorism.

A eulogy may include components of the classical *consolatio* style. This tendency is particularly evident in Robert Hassell's eulogy, written in response to a tragic, unexpected death. King's eulogy is another example. As he altered his eulogy for the bombing victims, King attenuated the deliberative aspects of the original speech and delivered a sermon more in line with the *consolatio* tradition. In fact, he added the conventional premise that all humans are mortal, albeit not in its traditional position at the beginning of the speech.

Since a eulogy is not a forensic speech designed to establish guilt or innocence, such a sermon generally does not attempt to defend the deity. Such defensiveness may detract from the hope and assurance that a funeral should provide. Consequently, very few funeral sermons focus on theodicy. I heard one preacher explain the term theodicy, note during his introduction that bad things may happen when people behave badly, and then continue with the body of his eulogy. In the current volume, only the King typescript includes a section on theodicy, and King omitted that section from the eulogy delivered a few days later.

The Eulogy in Logical Perspective

Logic addresses the question of how a speaker or writer communicates his/her major points. Generally, a funeral sermon situates the decedent's life and death and the continued existence and behavior of the bereaved in the larger perspective of the divine economy. The character of the eulogy as a praise/blame speech with the emphasis on praise facilitates this transition. Many forms of reasoning are available to help the eulogizer navigate from the immediacy of death to the divine purpose. However, the three most prevalent forms are deductive, dialectical, and inductive logic. Very few sermons utilize one type of reasoning to the exclusion of all others. Most rely on a dominant and one or more supporting logical strategies.

Deductive reasoning in its purest form progresses by logical steps from premise to conclusion. The initial premise is incontrovertible, and each subsequent step is a necessary subsequent to the prior step. The result of this progression is a conclusion that excludes all others. An example of such logic pertinent to funerals is 1 Corinthians 15, Paul's essay on the resurrection and afterlife. The success of Paul's logic with any reader, of course, depends on that reader's acceptance of the premise derived from Paul's Pharisaic training: The fact of Jesus' resurrection implies that the doctrine of the general resurrection is accurate (1 Cor. 15:12-20).

Dialectical reasoning is a variant of the deductive method. Peter M. Wherry advocates the use of Samuel

DeWitt Proctor's six-step dialectical outline in funerals for those who died under questionable circumstances or for deaths that may cause family members to question their faith.[28] Proctor's six-step model is useful as an outline for sermon preparation. However, the logic of the dialectical approach is considerably simpler. At its core, this approach requires the presentation of a pair of contradictory premises of comparable importance and plausibility. Each premise attenuates the other; with both premises in play, neither can be completely accurate or inaccurate. The tension between the two premises pushes the sermon toward a concluding synthesis which alleviates the dissonance. Both the King typescript and *I have a dream* exemplify dialectical logic; Proctor was one of King's mentors at Crozer.

Inductive reasoning cites multiple examples to lead the audience to a highly probable conclusion. In the event that counterexamples should be present, extraneous factors may explain them, or the counterexamples might not be sufficiently strong to shake the conclusion. Pompey's eulogy provides an interesting example of this technique. In the sermon, a list of good things the decedent did during his career as a blacksmith outweighs the single incident of larceny that sent him to the penitentiary. Furthermore, the example of Paul and Silas in jail and that of the crucified bandit blessed by Jesus reinforce the argument that neither incarceration nor criminal activity, *per se*, should be held to preclude eternal life.

---

[28] *Preaching Funerals in the Black Church: Bringing Perspective to Pain* (Valley Forge: Judson, 2013), 56-57.

Walking Beside Us in Our Sorrow:
Entry Points

A funeral sermon takes into account three factors. First, the entire service, including the eulogy, is undertaken for the benefit of the living. Thus, the minister must use all relevant resources to address their life situations. Second, the service memorializes the decedent. This task requires that the minister learn whatever s/he can about the decedent and use that information selectively in a speech that focuses on praise but does not ignore problematical behaviors. Third and most importantly, the eulogy memorializes the decedent for the benefit of the survivors by situating the decedent's beliefs, behavior, and future in the context of the Christian assurance of redemption for humans who are imperfect, yet still made in the image of God.

I once officiated a funeral and delivered a eulogy for a Caucasian decedent whose remains were buried in the coroner's cemetery. I considered it my responsibility to situate the decedent's life and death within the context of Christian hope by providing an honest witness to the high school students assisting with the ceremony. I used as my text the parable of the prodigal son (Luke 15:11-32). I noted that the decedent had damaged her health by drinking irresponsibly and smoking. I did not moralize about those activities but simply noted their effect on her health. I then spent the bulk of the sermon describing the way she came to her senses after an accident and realized that she needed to remain in the structured environment of a nursing home in order to avoid relapsing into her addictive behaviors. The parallels between the decedent's life story and the scripture passage were both obvious and fortunate.

Individuals' religious and spiritual practices, social ties, and other factors vary considerably. For that reason, what can be known about a decedent is unique to each situation. When a minister did not know the decedent, collateral information from the survivors can be immensely helpful. If nothing else, such information lets the eulogizer understand the ways the survivors already are beginning to interpret the decedent's life and place it in a larger context. McDonald's three variants illustrate the use of collateral information, and one of her longer works describes her procedure in more detail.[29]

In most cases, the eulogizer has some information about the decedent, either from that individual while s/he was alive or from collateral sources. In rare instances, one may be called upon to preach a commitment service for a set of unidentified remains or for someone who died alone, with no family or friends. In such not-always-hypothetical situations, the minister has a specific piece of information about the decedent. At life's conclusion, that individual was known only to God. With that information, abundant scriptural texts on abandonment, especially from the Psalms and gospel passion narratives, and thanks to those strangers who chose to memorialize the unknown decedent, sufficient

---

[29]*A prophetic witness in pastoral worship: Preaching funerals for Christians who are unknown to clergy*, D.Min. project, Louisville (KY) Presbyterian Theological seminary, 2016.

material exists to address all three points of entry. For this reason, I consider all funeral sermons eulogies and strive to address the decedent's life story, the survivors' life circumstances, and the Christian hope appropriately for each situation.

Various interpretive methods enable the eulogizer to engage the audience through the decedent's life story, the survivors' emerging interpretation of the decedent's life, or the Christian scriptural tradition. Among the methods that Wherry describes, verse-by-verse exposition of a scripture passage is primarily deductive, leading the audience inexorably to a conclusion necessitated by the premise that the passage, as scripture, is authoritative. Of course, this method uses the Christian scriptural tradition as its entry point. However, an effective exposition depends on the realistic connection of the scripture passage to the other two entry points. In contrast, the application method begins with the listeners' life circumstances. A series of questions relates those circumstances to relevant scripture passages, and the decedent's life story might serve as an informative example.[30] This approach is largely inductive. A well-known example is Jesus' warning in Luke 13:1-5.

In one sense, African Americans and Caucasians have lived in close proximity in the United States and have taught each other some of their customs for the past four centuries. In another sense, however, they have lived side-by-side, frequently in separate communities, and have

---

[30]Wherry, *Preaching Funerals in the Black Church*, 54-56.

developed their own social mores. Both the shared and the unique dimensions of their experience have influenced each decedent's life story, each survivor's interpretation of the death, and the ways in which Christian scripture is used to situate death within a larger, more hopeful context. At this point, we illustrate some African American approaches to the funeral sermon by presenting exemplary eulogies from African American clergy and other prominent speakers.

2

Can You See Yourself Being There One Day?

WINSTON GEORGE BENNETT, III
CHRIST TEMPLE CHRISTIAN LIFE CENTER
LOUISVILLE, KY

Telling and retelling the story of a decedent's impact frequently helps the bereft come to terms with the death and move forward productively. When a close friend or relative of a decedent is capable of delivering a coherent eulogy, the funeral can play an early but important role in this process. In such a situation, a minister may serve the bereft simply by providing a time and place for them to situate the deceased within the larger Christian story. The minister himself or herself may officiate, keep the service on track, and say very little. The funeral of Winston George Bennett, Jr. was such an occasion. His son, who has done some writing and motivational speaking, provided an implied comparison of the decedent with Paul. This early missionary and writer considered himself a master builder of faith communities that followed Christ in such a manner as to permit participation by Jews and Gentiles alike. Likewise, the eulogizer characterized his father, apparently a brick mason, as a builder who prepared his children to succeed at their various, adult endeavors. Thus, the comparison included the decedent's occupation as well as his family.

Thanks to Troy Taylor for recording and to rev.com for transcribing this eulogy.

> According to God's grace that he has given me, as a wise builder, I have laid a foundation on which others are building. Let each one pay attention to the way he builds. (1 Cor. 3:10)

... over this door. I was about probably his height. I was like this. Every day, two hours a day, I would jump and try to block those darn shots. How good was I when I first started, you think? Not good. But that shot blocking at six took me to the NBA[1] at 24. You know what I'm saying? He had this to say to me ... He would always say this. He'd say, "Winston ...." We'd be watching Louisville play on TV because I'm a huge Louisville fan too, even though I went to Kentucky. Speaking of which, my

---

[1] National Basketball Association, where the eulogizer played briefly for the Cleveland Cavaliers and served briefly as an assistant coach with the Boston Celtics.

daughter's coaches are in the back, so I want to recognize them, the UofL[2] volleyball team coaches, and the great season that they had.

But he would always say ..., he would say, "Winston, can you see yourself being there one day?" I'm six or seven years old. I can't possibly see myself 18 years down the road. I didn't realize what he was doing, but he was giving me a vision at six years old. He was a master builder. Here was a guy who would get up at five AM every morning and go to Louisville Brick and Block. He made block for a living for about 25 years. After giving 25 years of his life, he comes in and gives a pink sheet and says the business is closing down. It's done. Every winter he would be laid off. As already has been stated, my father was stubborn, and he was a big man. I would always get on him about how loud he would be talking to my mother.

This is when I was about six, because every Friday I knew they were going to sit at the kitchen table, and they were going to talk about the bills. He used to tell me: "I'm 500 pounds, how you expect me to talk like a mouse? I ain't no mouse. Even if I talk normal it's like a lion coming out. Rawr." I said, "Man you got a point. You've got a point there." He would ask me all the time, "Can you see yourself being there?" That stretched me so much. There were times ..., I'll be honest with you, there were times I didn't like my father. That's how hard he was on me in terms of practice.

[2]Universityof Louisville.

Whenever I played a game, if I had ten rebounds he asked, "Why didn't you bring 20 rebounds in here? You had ten. You didn't play the second half? He was always pushing me and I didn't understand when I was young. Once I got to a point where I could understand that, I sat one day, and I just cry because I just couldn't see how this man could live such selfless life. See, what you don't know is that he made it only to about the tenth or eleventh grade. He had parents who were always sickly. His brothers and sisters are here today. My extended family..., and all of them are here today, which I love, and I appreciate you.

He said, because his parents couldn't support him, he was about 6'4", 350 walking up and down the halls of Jeffersonville High School.... Football coach comes up to him and said, "Boy you ever played football?" He said, "No sir, never played football." The coach said, "I want you to come out and play football." So my father found his way out to the football field, started to play, started popping people. He didn't know nothing about football, but there was one thing missing. He had nobody there to say, "Man, you're doing good. Keep hitting them. Keep going to practice, arrive early, stay late," because his parents were sick. What was it nine, eight, nine of y'all? That's a lot of mouths to feed, so he had to drop out of school in the tenth, eleventh grade, go work on the highways to bring some money into the house.

So he said, if I ever have a son I'm going to be at every game I can. I'm going to be at every practice and I'm going to push him to the hill. Whatever success I've ever obtained is due to him and due to my first mother. You see, I'm such a handful, God said, "I need to give you two mothers." Mother Jennings has been a spitting image of..., let me tell you. She told me one day. She said, "I'm going to have to jack some people up because they were talking about you." Let me tell you now, if you smile in front of my face, if you're talking about me and she hears it, oh it's on. It's on, so you better be real.

She loves us that much, and I love you and I appreciate you. Master builder is the thing that I want to leave you with and leaving you with this. There was an old Indian man whose only responsibility was take this water to the king of India. Everyday he'd walk five or six miles to the river, fill up these big jars of water, had the bamboo on his back so he's carrying water like this [demonstrates the walk]. Five miles! This man is old but he continued to strive. He continued to carry the water. That means he was pushing himself. That means he was doing it when he didn't want to do it. That means he was getting up and going to work when he didn't feel like it. That means he went to practice when he might have been hurting, but he kept doing it. He kept doing it.

So he got to the palace. One of the jars of water said, I'm so thankful that you chose me because I give good clean water to the king. He was happy about it. The other big pail of water was complaining. You see, the other pail of water, by the time it got to the king, there was very little left because that pail had cracks in it. So that pail would always feel like it had been abused and always feel like life had treated him so unfairly. So the next time they walked to the king and he got some water, he went to the river and got some water, started making the five mile trip, and here go the pails.

The pails were talking to each other. I'm the bad pail. I'm the good pail. They had bad and good. I'm the bad pail. I get to carry the king the whole thing of water. Here's the other pail. I don't have much to give a king. I've got cracks. In this story, really the master builder was the old man carrying the water. He said, "Look here, you're a good pail because you carried the king lots of water. But he said to the pail with the cracks, you a great pail also. He said, "I bet you haven't noticed as we walked these five miles to the king's place. Have you looked down beside the road to see all the flowers growing on your side? The only reason they're growing is that your cracks have watered them and allowed them to grow."

See, we ain't got no excuse. I've got plenty of cracks, but I still got a responsibility to make some things grow in my life. I ain't got it all together, but he told me never to give up. He told me to keep getting up and going to practice even when I didn't feel like it. He told me to go to class when I didn't feel like getting the grades. He said, "Keep watering." We got a great cloud of witnesses that tells us to keep watering no matter what we go through.[3] Between him and my mother,…, and now Ms. Carla James,

---

[3] Hebrews 12:1

I've got some watering to do. But not me only. We all left here together. We've seen ..., and I don't know why I forget or why we forget. Don't you know we're on the same team?

What you going through I'm, going through too more than likely. At the end of the day, whether you're bishop, whether you're the ushers, we all got problems. We all got issues. Will somebody please pass the tissues. That's one of bishops saying. So I want to thank everybody here today for allowing ..., for just coming man, for showing love. If you sent a text—I got so many social media replies and all that stuff—it all means something. Don't undervalue your voice in encouraging somebody else because we all got this journey to travel through. We can just encourage someone instead of criticizing him when they go through.

I always tell my kids this. Whenever you criticize somebody else, you've got one finger pointed at them, but you've got three pointing back at yourself. Keep that in mind because at the end of the day He's the greatest. We're from this earthy dirt and to this dirt we shall return.[4] With money, no money, with wins, with losses, we're going to the grave unless he takes us up from here. Love you very much. Thank you so much. Thank all of you. God bless you.

---

[4]Genesis 3:19.

The entrance to Christ Temple Christian Life Center, Louisville, KY, with the flags of several nations displayed beneath a large cross.

3

A Blessed Man

GEORGE AND SHIRLEY BURKE
COKE MEMORIAL UNITED METHODIST CHURCH
LOUISVILLE, KY

George Burke, assisted by his wife Shirley preached the following sermon. The occasion was the funeral of a long-term member of the congregation that they co-pastor. The decedent, here called John Doe, died suddenly. On the one hand, he seemed reasonably healthy, so his death was unexpected. On the other hand, he was almost ninety years of age. Thus he and his fellow congregants were aware that he was approaching a stage during which his grip on life might become increasingly tenuous.

   Mr. Doe was "a man of sorrows, acquainted with grief."[1] Two of his three children predeceased him. He

---

[1] Isaiah 53:3

did have a family though. He was survived by his wife, a daughter, and several extended family members. In addition, he remained an active in his church family until the end of his life. In fact, on the Saturday that he died, he had prepared already to attend Sunday School the next day.

In this context, the funeral was structured as a celebration of life. In fact, in his introduction, George Burke alluded to the "homegoing" aspect of the service. The sermon was a eulogy, depicting the decedent as a positive example of Christian behavior, worthy of emulation. The text, Psalm 1, provided an outline and a sub-structure for the elaboration of the decedent's life as an example. This example led to a brief discussion of the larger context of the Christian hope for eternal life in the presence of the Lord. The sermon concluded with an invitation, presumably followed by an opportunity for those present to make public professions of Christian faith.

Coke Memorial United Methodist Church, Louisville, KY.

Psalm 1 (NIV)
¹Blessed is the one who does not walk in step with the wicked or stand in the way that sinners take or sit in the company of mockers, ²but whose delight is in the law of the Lord, and who meditates on his law day and night. ³That person is like a tree planted by streams of water, which yields its fruit in season and whose leaf does not wither—whatever they do prospers. ⁴Not so the wicked! They are like chaff that the wind blows away. ⁵Therefore the wicked will not stand in judgement, nor sinners in the assembly of the righteous. ⁶For the Lord watches over the way of the righteous, but the way of the wicked leads to destruction.

Psalm 1 was Brother Doe's favorite passage of scripture. The psalm begins with a blessing, which we define as follows: Blessed means to speak well of or to have the favor of God. We would like to share briefly with you (1) what a blessed man does not do, (2) what a blessed man does, (3) what a blessed man yields, and (4) the reward of a blessed man.

In verses 1 and 2, we have the things that a blessed man does not do: (1) Walk in the counsel of the ungodly, (2) stand in the way of sinners, and (3) sit in the seat of the scornful.

Brother John Doe had his car gassed up to go the Sunday School the day before the Lord called him home. He rarely missed church, and he was the first student at Sunday School and mid-week Bible study. He believed in being on time. He said to me Sunday before last, "When a man stops learning, he is done." He had firm biblical convictions and was never wishy-washy. He called sin—Sin. I never heard him criticize or scorn anyone. He spoke words of life and hope. Walking in the counsel of the ungodly, standing in the way of sinners, and sitting in the seat of the scornful was just not his way!

In verse 2, we have the things that a blessed man does: (1) Delights in the law of the Lord and (2) Meditates day and night.

Brother Doe loved the word and pondered many a deep subject that many never even considered. Although his sight had diminished with age, you often could see him moving his lips when the scriptures were read. That required meditation.

In verse 3, we have what a blessed man yields.

Like a tree planted by streams of water. Strong connection to the source of life Brother Doe was a man of prayer.

Yields its fruit in season. Almost 70 years of marriage. I noticed in life there is a glow on a woman's face at three different times: (a) at salvation, (b) when carrying a child, and (c) loved by her husband. The glow on Sister Doe's face demonstrates she is loved. The fact that Brother Doe loved his family is very evident as well.

Leaf does not wither. Brother Doe's legacy of his testimony continues to live on.

Whatever he does prospers. Encouragement goes a long way. I have heard how generations of people young and old would make a special effort to ensure that they spoke to Brother Doe after each church service at Cooke. He was well loved and respected by the members of his church. And Brother Doe truly loved his church. He had a wealth of wisdom and lavished encouragement on so many people.

Verses 4 and 5 contrast the plight of the wicked with the status of the blessed. The more time one spends with God, the more one becomes concerned about the things God cares about. Brother Doe was very much concerned about the lost in his circle of contacts. He knew that the wicked are like the chaff which the wind blows away and that the wicked shall not stand in the judgement, nor sinners in the assembly of the righteous. And because Brother Doe had the heart of God, he, like God, didn't want anyone to perish!

Finally, in verse 6, the psalm speaks of the respective rewards of the righteous and the wicked. The Lord watches over the way of the righteous. Brother Doe knew from scripture that it might be preferable to be absent from the body and present with the Lord.[2] By experience, he admitted that there is a time, purpose, and season for everything, a time to be born and a time to die.[3] Through his suffering, he came to the realization that God works all things together for the good of those who love him.[4] In

---

[2] 2 Corinthians 5:8

[3] Ecclesiastes 3:1-2.

[4] Romans 8:28.

summary, he know that God uses the best possible means to get the best possible results for the greatest number of people for the longest period of time, every time. God is sovereign. He knows what is best, and Brother Doe trusted his God!

The life lived well by Brother Doe incarnated the portions of Psalm 1 that address the status of the righteous. Brother Doe embodied the example of the teaching and preaching of God's word and the power of the Holy Spirit.

Brother John Doe is in the presence of the Lord. In the presence of the Lord is the fullness of joy.[5]

For those who have not yet received Jesus as your Savior, won't you consider him today?

---

[5]Psalm 16:11.

4

A Culminating Conversation!

ROBERT O'KEEFE HASSELL
KINGDOM LOVE WORSHIP CENTER
MADISON, TN

A death which is premature, tragic, or unexpected likely will accentuate perceptions among the bereft that the circumstances are progressing beyond human control. In funerals generally, but especially when faced with an unusually vexing death, the minister may acknowledge the evident lack of human control and then countervail this observation with an assurance of divine control that surpasses even death. Robert Hassell's eulogy takes such an approach by examining Jesus' comportment during his crucifixion. The sermon argues that Jesus, the seeming victim, was in control of the situation. Hassell's Jesus was aware of the prophecies regarding the coming messiah and pursued those prophecies to their excruciating completion.

Hassell exhibits an interest in tradition to promote the perception that the bereft are regaining control in spite of the situation. Comfort food at the repast and familiar liturgical elements during the service may have contributed to this impression. During the sermon, the consistent use of the 1611 Authorized (King James) translation provides scriptural citation in a form familiar to individuals raised in a wide variety of English-speaking churches.

In his transcription, Hassell has used various sorts of print emphasis to indicate the points he emphasized verbally during the sermon. I have retained this emphasis to suggest to readers the way the eulogy was delivered.

> "When Jesus therefore had received the vinegar, he said, It is finished: and he bowed his head, and gave up the ghost." (John 19:30)

Here, we see in John's account the final moments leading up to Christ's final physical demise, crucified alongside common criminals. It is John's Gospel which most emphatically underscores the fulfillment of prophecy in the events surrounding our Lord's death. Death on the cross was shameful, excruciating, and often protracted.[1]

---

[1] From a Jewish perspective, Deuteronomy 21:23 labeled as accursed those executed by methods that involved hanging or whose corpses were displayed on a tree or pole. In 1 Corinthians 1:23, Paul labeled the proclamation of a crucified messiah offensive to Jews and ludicrous to heathen. Semahot 2:11 advised the relatives of crucifixion victims to move to a different locale or, if they lived in one of the empire's larger cities, to the opposite side of town. For additional information on the

Even in the middle of what appears to be defeat, victory remains present. Jesus knew that everything had been completed. He was no helpless victim! He was not powerless, but very much in control. All eyes in this moment are on Jesus. While those who are under authority to administer and execute him appear to be in control, they are yet under subjection. Jesus was aware of every Scripture that spoke of his atoning death as the promised Messiah.

As we assemble today to celebrate this life, there may be poignant questions surrounding this death, coupled with difficult feelings concerning its unexpected nature. We find ourselves in shock and overwhelming disbelief and even may experience having our faith shaken to the core concerning the undeniable facts that are in front of us today. The word of God comes to remind us this afternoon that although we may have human moments, we are not without hope! Today, family and friends, while confronted with this difficult time of transition in the life of the departed, some of you may think that death has won. You may be under the assumption that death has singlehandedly dealt a crushing blow to you and your loved one in an unfair way. Despite what this looks like right now, the certainty is that death has already hit you with its best shot,

---

stigma attached to crucifixion in antiquity, see Martin Hengel, *Crucifixion in the ancient world and the folly of the message of the cross*, tr. John Bowden (Philadelphia: Fortress, 1977).

yet remains defeated. It may look as if this moment is <u>HANDLING YOU</u>, but God is <u>HANDLING IT</u>, whatever your <u>IT</u> might be. The things that come along with this very moment that you are presently facing cannot go any farther than God allows. Death, although an adversary, is a measure of assistance to the believer to get to the next level. Charles Spurgeon said, "The best moment of a Christian's life is his last one, because it is the one that is nearest Heaven. And then it is that he begins to strike the keynote of the song which he shall sing to all eternity."[2]

Moving forward, as I contemplated the reality of sorrow that we see today, I looked at the text and I saw something that is critical to our understanding of this difficult situation. That there was something in the text became very clear to me. Two quick points our text makes will assist us as we transition from sorrow to victory.

➢ The CYCLE has been INTERRUPTED!

Since the original sin of Lucifer's rebellion in heaven and the subsequent sin of our species through Adam, humankind has entered into a vicious cycle. It took a place called Calvary to bring this cycle to a conclusion. It all ended with a simple 3-word statement: IT IS FINISHED! A cycle, by definition, is a series of events repeated regularly in the same order. Sin had created a cycle, which can be seen in the face of our present sufferings and trials. Some of us walked in here this afternoon in the middle of a

---

[2] https://www.viralbeliever.com/christian-quotes-about-death-afterlife/ (accessed 06/29/2019).

cycle! Wondering when will life change for the better? When will it stop? Will my life ever come together? Will I ever find forgiveness? Does God really love me? In the text, we see Jesus interrupt the cycle through an intentional interjection for the sake of an eternal intervention! The Bible says in Romans 6:9, *"Knowing that Christ, having been raised from the dead, is never to die again; death no longer is master over Him."* The death of Christ served its purpose effectively. Its goal was to purchase not only the completeness of salvation but also reconciliation for a people who belonged to him. For the bible says in Psalm 24:1, *"The earth is the LORD'S, and the fulness thereof; the world, and they that dwell therein."* Jesus teaches us that interventions and interruptions oftentimes are inconvenient! Death is an intervention! Death is an interruption! Death is inconvenient! It comes with a cost, but it is for a cause! The picture we see in front of us today is a place of inconvenience within our humanity, but a costly intervention has already been made for the cause of a better outcome. The good news this afternoon, for those of you who yet remain alive, is that Jesus has come to break the cycle over your life! Which means you do not have to LIVE IN IT, SUFFER WITH IT, and CONTINUE TO CARRY IT or be OVERTAKEN by IT! The cycle has been broken! For the Bible says in 1 Corinthians 15:20 -26

> *But now is Christ risen from the dead, and become the first fruits of them that slept. For since by*

man came death, by man came also the resurrection of the dead. For as in Adam all die, even so in Christ shall all be made alive. But every man in his own order: Christ the first fruits; afterward they that are Christ's at his coming. Then cometh the end, when he shall have delivered up the kingdom to God, even the Father; when he shall have put down all rule and all authority and power. For he must reign, till he hath put all enemies under his feet. The last enemy that shall be destroyed is death. For he hath put all things under his feet. But when he saith, all things are put under him, it is manifest that he is excepted, which did put all things under him. And when all things shall be subdued unto him, then shall the Son also himself be subject unto him that put all things under him, that God may be all in all."

Touch your neighbor, encourage them and tell them, "The cycle has been broken and it is all under control!"

➢ Jesus has SET the RECORD STRAIGHT!

Death is a difficult space, even for believers, because we struggle with handling the separation from the physical existence of the people that we love and cherish. We desire closure. Many of us feel as though closure is evasive, owing to the way the transition occurred. Nevertheless, there is a measure of clarity that becomes clearer with time as we continue to journey forward.

A conversation is an interactive communication among two or more people. The development of conversational skills and etiquette is an important part of socialization. In conversation, dialogue goes better if both conversational partners understand the purpose of the conversation. Think for a moment about the reason we talk. There is always a combination of explanations behind every conversation. It could be anything from making a plan or discussing a problem to just getting to know someone better. The Bible says in Proverbs 4:7, *"Wisdom is the principal thing; therefore get wisdom: and with all thy getting get understanding."* If there is a lack of understanding, a miscommunication is likely to occur that leads to a place of misunderstanding.

We all know something about misunderstandings and miscommunications. These situations can create places of strife, cause people to have wayward dispositions and create a climate of conflict. The most common causes of misunderstanding and miscommunication are assumptions and hasty communication. However, nothing eliminates miscommunication like a concrete clarification. People will judge you for one mistake! Folks will start writing you off as a person, owing to their perceptions of your temporary circumstances. They talk about you on the basis of what they heard from another person secondhand! Nevertheless, there is a man who has set the record straight concerning your life! The Bible says in John 8:32, *"And ye shall know the truth, and the truth shall make you free."*

I am so glad that the God I serve has a solution to every place of speculation.

Here I must pause to address an issue concerning the text, which will rebuke a spirit of hopelessness when it comes to dealing with the harsh reality that death brings to our lives. Notice in the text, that Jesus did not say, "I AM FINISHED!" – He said "IT IS FINISHED!" I know that looking at this casket and flowers in front of you is difficult to process. Some of you walked in this building today thinking that all was lost and today would be the end of the person lying in front of you. Today, I have come to let you know that Jesus said, "IT IS FINISHED!" Therefore, the person lying in front of you IS NOT FINISHED!

The reason is that if he had said, "I AM FINISHED!" – He would have invalidated his statement concerning his identification. Contrary to popular speculation and assumption, he was not by himself on the cross that day. The Bible says in John 10:30, *"I and my Father are one."*

If he had said, "I AM FINISHED!" – It would have further indicated the nullification of God's statement in Exodus 3:14 when he spoke out of a bush that was on fire because there was a necessity to reveal himself: *"And God said unto Moses. I AM THAT I AM: and he said, thus shalt thou say unto the children of Israel, I AM hath sent me unto you."*

If he had said, "I AM FINISHED!" – John's statement in John 1:1-4 would have been annulled that says

"In the beginning was the Word, and the Word was with God, and the Word was God. The same was in the beginning with God. All things were made by him; and without him was not anything made that was made. In him was life; and the life was the light of men."

Subsequently, the recantation or retraction of that statement would have made him a liar. – But Numbers 23:19 says, *"God is not a man that he should lie; neither the son of man, that he should repent: hath he said, and shall he not do it? Or hath he spoken, and shall he not make it good?"* This causes me to conclude that God cannot lie about himself. That same God cannot lie about what he said concerning you either! This is why he said "IT IS FINISHED!" and "I AM NOT FINISHED!" He was speaking to a myriad of situations, like the one we are confronted with today, to let us know that even death has an expiration date! Just wave your Holy Ghost filled hand in your neighbor's direction and declare, "God is just getting started!"

As I take my leave this afternoon, it is my job to preach the Gospel in the face of Death, to convict the living and revive their hope. I want to end by saying the following: There was serious misunderstanding at Calvary that day that needed to be resolved! Apparently, someone forgot the memo that Jesus issued in John 12:32, *"And I, if I be lifted up from the earth, will draw all men unto me."* There was some confusion among entities that were not in plain sight or visible to the human eye. Satan, Death and Time were spectators on Calvary that day. The three of them had opinions about Jesus' condition and the final outcome. The rumor among the three of them was that they had Jesus "in the bag" and the "deal was sealed!" Satan said, "We got him right where we want him!" Death said, "This is the end." Time said, "There is no coming back from this!" Some of you have heard these exact same things said to you in your life! It was here Jesus raised himself up a sixth time to set the record straight! Creation had been disconnected and separated from God since the Fall of Adam. God had not spoken for four hundred years between the Old and the New Testaments. Satan is the Accuser of man! Death is the Adversary of man! Time is the Administrator of the physical penalty regarding the sin of man! When Jesus said, "It Is Finished," he informed SATAN of his DESTINATION. He spoke to DEATH concerning his DISPOSITION and he informed TIME of his LIMITATION! This means for everybody that Satan, Death and Time will not be the end of you! The Bible says in 1 Corinthians 15:54, *"So when this corruptible shall have put on incorruption, and this mortal shall have put on immortality, then shall be brought to pass the saying that is written, Death is swallowed up in victory."* Jesus set the record straight! For those of you who must walk away from this situation today, whatever they said or could say does not even matter! Every label has been lifted! Every rumor has been removed! In the end, we still win!

"It is finished" is the culminating conversation that guarantees that what God said concerning you has to happen! Everything surrounding this situation today has already been resolved. For the Bible says in Philippians 1:6, *"Being confident of this very thing, that he which hath begun a good work in you will perform it until the day of Jesus Christ."* I am so glad that the God I serve is a FINISHER! He has FINISHED this situation in front of us! He has FINISHED ME! He is FINISHING YOU! The Bible says in Job 23:10 says, *"But he knoweth the way that I take: when he hath tried me, I shall come forth as gold."* You are going to LIVE and you will LIVE AGAIN, because IT IS FINISHED! You are going to OVERCOME, because IT IS FINISHED! I thank God today, because this conversation is the final verdict on my condition and conclusion. This is why we can proclaim today, in the face of death, that it will not end like this!

Zion Baptist Church, Inc., Louisville, KY. Gerald J. Joiner is the current pastor. One of his predecessors was Albert Daniel Williams King, the brother of Martin Luther King, Jr.

5

A Mighty Man of Valor: Eulogy for Taurean Delon Joiner

GERALD J. JOINER
ZION BAPTIST CHURCH, INC.
LOUISVILLE, KY

To the extent that death is regarded as a normal conclusion to life, it is normal statistically for children to outlive and bury their parents. When an untimely death precipitates a reversal of these roles, the survivors may experience the death as unusually traumatic. Gerald and Luevern Joiner faced this situation as they supported their son through his final battle with metastatic colon cancer. Like other bereaved individuals, the Joiners had to manage their own grief and mourning. By virtue of his pastoral role, Gerald Joiner was responsible not only for his own bereavement process but also for supporting grief-stricken parishioners and other acquaintances. Furthermore, the responsibility of church leadership remained ever-present, even with the difficult personal/family circumstance.

The eulogy attends to both the behavioral and the emotional dimensions of the family's bereavement. The eulogy describes the family's wondering why the terminal cancer occurred, prayers for miraculous healing, and concern that their Christian commitment might have been inadequate. These perceptions fit neatly within Elisabeth Kübler-Ross' five stages of anticipatory grief (denial and isolation, anger, bargaining, depression, acceptance).[1] Kübler-Ross extrapolated these stages out of material gleaned from interviews with terminally ill patients, many with cancer. Thus, the stage theory is appropriate logically for the anticipatory grief that friends and relatives might experience as they process the experience parallel to and in dialogue with the dying individual.

The eulogy provides evidence not only of emotional but also of behavioral responses to bereavement. Joiner focused on the eulogy and let H. D. Cockerham, his retired predecessor, keep the service as a whole on track. This focus provided a specific response to the bereavement and enabled Joiner to continue leading in worship, even during his difficult circumstance.

Joiner predicated the eulogy on the metaphor of a military campaign. This imagery portrays cancer as an implacable enemy, courses of treatment and the procedures included in those courses as strategies and tactics, and

---

[1] *On death and dying: What the dying have to teach doctors, nurses, clergy, and their own families* (New York: MacMillan, 1964).

Taurean as a brave warrior who had to battle cancer. A prayer that Douglas MacArthur is said to have written during his first Pacific campaign punctuates the eulogy and drives home the metaphor.

MacArthur's first Pacific campaign failed. Two years later, MacArthur returned to the Phillipines and led a second, successful campaign. Likewise, Taurean Joiner's battle with cancer ended unsuccessfully in the sense that cancer killed him. However, the eulogy moved quickly from that result to the Christian assurance that, for a Christian, death is neither final nor definitive. Thus the eulogy transports its audience from the heartache of their current situation to a proleptic view of the Christian's ultimate destiny.

To Pastor Emeritus H. D. Cockerham, who is officiating this homegoing celebration,

To my brother in the ministry, Pastor Joseph Owens of Shiloh Baptist Church Lexington KY, who spoke on behalf of all the clergy present,

To all other Pastors, Assistant Pastors, Associate Ministers and religious laity,

To the deacons, trustees, spiritual officers, auxiliary leaders and members of this great church, Zion Baptist Church Inc.,

To this bereaved family, my family, my daughter Jon'a, my beautiful granddaughter Zoe, my son Gemayel,

To all my brothers and sisters, nephews and nieces, great nephews and nieces, cousins, extended family members, and friends of Taurean and Jon'a,

I bring you greetings and prayerful words of comfort from the spirit filled saints of Zion Baptist Church, Inc. where I have the blessed privilege of serving as Pastor and under-shepherd.

Before I preach, I'd like to take this opportunity as Taurean's father to express my personal appreciation to a number of people who have played a special role in my son's life over the past few years:

1. To Pastor Dave Stone, the Bible study class and members of Southeast Christian Church who have helped shape the spiritual growth of my son, over the last few years, thank you,
2. To Dr. Woodcock, Tasha and the entire nursing staff of Norton's Cancer Center on east Broadway, who have lovingly ministered to my son through carefully administering chemotherapy to him over the past seven years, thank you,
3. To the entire nursing staff, graduate fellows and medical assistants of Dr. Robert Martin who work on the fifth floor of Norton's hospital downtown where they repeatedly provided emergency medical care to my son each time we encountered a crises during his seven-year battle with cancer, thank you,
4. To his employer, The Apple Corporation... and the local management team of the Oxmoor Retail

outlet... thank you for your compassionate understanding, acceptance, support and grace during the time Taurean needed to take medical leave or short term disability, thank you,

5. To the members of Zion... for all the cards and prayers that you've lifted for my son... but especially for giving your pastor the emotional support and necessary time off every other Friday over the last seven years so that I could spend time supporting Taurean during his chemo sessions, thank you,

6. And finally, to my daughter Jon'a F. Joiner: As I have stated privately and also publically, thank you for your undying love, support, encouragement and care of my son over the past seven years. I believe Taurean would not have made it this long without you. Thank you!

There is a word found in two particular passages of scripture from the Old Testament that I find to be quite apropos in describing my son Taurean. The first passage is 1 Samuel 16:18 and the second is 1 Chronicles: 12:8.

1 Samuel 16:18 reads: *Then one of the young men said, "Behold, I have seen a son of Jesse the Bethlehemite who is a skillful musician,* a mighty man of valor, *a warrior, one prudent in speech, and a handsome man; and the* LORD *is with him."*

1 Chronicles 12:8 reads: *From the Gadites there came over to David in the stronghold in the wilderness,* mighty men of valor, *men trained for war, who could handle shield and spear, and whose faces were like the faces of lions, and they were as swift as the gazelles on the mountains.*

From these two texts, I want to speak on the subject of: *"A Mighty Man of Valor"* and offer up as a supposition the fact that my son, Taurean Delon Joiner, was a *"Mighty Man of Valor."*

Now the American Heritage Dictionary defines valor as; *Courage and boldness, as in battle,* and Dictionary.com defines valor as *boldness of determination in facing great danger, especially in battle; heroic courage; and or bravery.* Those of you who really knew my son knew that he continuously demonstrated courage and bravery. He exhibited a boldness of determination in facing the great mystery/danger of cancer. If you had any interaction at all with Taurean, you couldn't help but describe him as being heroic and courageous in the way that he approached his condition. Whenever you asked him how he was doing, his instantaneous response was, "I'm doing fine; I won't complain!"

When we first learned of his cancer seven years ago, his mother Luevern and I were devastated. We collectively prayed for God's miraculous healing. We queried the Lord as to why this would happen to our son and repeatedly begged the Lord for His intervention and healing. Although we kept up the outer appearance of confidence, we both secretly feared for our son's life and wondered whether or not his cancer was due to anything we had done. Had our Christian commitment been suspect? Had it been too weak? *Was it all in vain?* Had we wasted our time bringing him up in the fear and admonition of the Lord, only to have the Lord desert him at this critical time of need? It was in this spirit of fear and contemplative prayer that the Lord led us to a particular prayer from General Douglas MacArthur that I have held onto for seven years now:

- Build me a son, O Lord, who will be strong enough to know when he is weak, and brave enough to face himself when he is afraid; one who will be proud and unbending in honest defeat, and humble and gentle in victory.
- Build me a son whose wishes will not take the place of deeds; a son who will know Thee—and that to know himself is the foundation stone of knowledge.
- Lead him, I pray, not in the path of ease and comfort, but under the stress and spur of difficulties and challenge. Here let him learn to stand up in the storm; here let him learn compassion for those who fail.
- Build me a son whose heart will be clear, whose goal will be high; a son who will master himself before he seeks to master other men; one who will reach into the future, yet never forget the past.
- And after all these things are his, add, I pray O Lord, enough of a sense of humor, so that he may

> always be serious, yet never take himself too seriously. Give him humility, so that he may always remember the simplicity of true greatness, the open mind of true wisdom and the meekness of true strength.
> - Then I his father, will dare to whisper, "I have not lived in vain."[2]

Those of you who knew Taurean could say that neither I, his father, nor Luevern, his mother, lived in vain, for he did indeed exemplify the type of son for whom General Douglas MacArthur prayed.

But now, let's get back to our texts. In both these texts, we find stories about individuals who were confronted with terrible situations—tremendous obstacles that they had to face, devastating odds that threatened to wipe out their very existence—yet they courageously faced those odds and miraculously overcame obstacles which others thought were impossible.

In the first scripture we learn of David's being chosen and anointed by God to replace King Saul.

Because of the prophet Samuel's obedience in following the commands of the Lord, we now have the adage, *you can't judge a book by its cover*, in other words, *you can't*

---

[2] New *York Times*, April 6, 1964: (https://www.newyorktimes.com/1964/04/06/archives/macarthur-leaves-a-spiritual-legacy-prayer-for-his-son.html, accessed 02/09/2019). This digitized version, printed originally the day after MacArthur's death, cites Courtney Whitney, McArthur's biographer and confidant, as claiming that McArthur wrote the prayer during his first, unsuccessful Pacific campaign.

judge whether or not a book is good simply by looking at its cover. Samuel passed over ten other sons of Jesse before he selected and anointed David. 1 Samuel 16:7 reads, *"Look not on his countenance, or on the height of his stature: because I have refused him: for the Lord seeth not as man seeth; for man looketh on the outward appearance, but the Lord looketh on the heart!"* In other words, man does not see what the Lord sees. Man sees what is visible, but the Lord sees what is invisible. The Lord sees what's in the heart! The Lord saw that David's heart was good and that he had demonstrated courage and bold determination in protecting his father's sheep from the lion and the bear. David won the favor of King Saul and became a permanent placement in his administration. God also put him in place to face and defeat the terrible giant of a man named Goliath. While others feared Goliath and wouldn't go out to challenge him, David called him an uncircumcised Philistine and told him in verses 45-47; *"You come to me with a sword, a spear, and a javelin, but I come to you in the name of the LORD of hosts, the God of the armies of Israel, whom you have taunted. "This day the LORD will deliver you up into my hands, and I will strike you down and remove your head from you. And I will give the dead bodies of the army of the Philistines this day to the birds of the sky and the wild beasts of the earth, that all the earth may know that there is a God in Israel, and that all this assembly may know that the LORD does not deliver by sword or by spear; for the battle is the LORD'S and He will give you into our hands."* David slew Goliath with a sling shot and a stone, cut off his head and then routed the whole Philistine army, all because of the fact that in his heart he was a mighty man of valor!

In the second scripture, 1 Chronicles 12:8, we learn of 11 men of valor who risked their lives to help David unite the kingdom and become King over all of Jerusalem. In one instance, three of them risked their lives by overcoming insurmountable odds. They broke through a large number of Philistines just so they could draw water out of the well of Bethlehem and present it to King David. They were men of might, and men of war fit for the battle, that could handle shield and buckler, whose faces were as swift as the roes upon the mountains!

What are you saying preacher? I'm simply saying that when they followed the *"man of valor"* they too became *"men of valor"* and were able to accomplish great feats of courage by showing a *boldness of determination especially in facing great danger, and battle!*

What does all this have to do with Taurean? Why Reverend, do you see him as a mighty man of valor? Well, just like David, Taurean had beautiful eyes and a healthy handsome appearance. Just like David, he was an obedient son and did everything his father told him to do.

Just like David, when he was confronted with insurmountable odds, he did not back down. Rather, he faced them boldly and depended on his God to deliver him through each one of them! Just like David, when they told him that he had colon cancer and that it had metastasized to his liver, he told his Goliath named Cancer that he came in the name of the Lord of hosts, the God of the children of Israel, and that God would deliver victory into his hands. He would not die!

Just like David, when they told him that his bile duct had collapsed and that he had a hernia and that they would have to go back in and do another surgery to fix it, he said go ahead. *"I shall not fear for the God I serve will deliver me so that all the earth may know that there is a God in Israel."*

Just like David, when they told Taurean that they could no longer use oxeleplatin or 5FU to target his tumor and that they would have to use another experimental chemical, Taurean said go ahead and use it *"so that all this assembly may know that the LORD God does not deliver by sword or by spear; for the battle is the LORD'S and He will give this cancer over into our hands."*

Yes, my son was a mighty man of valor who trusted in the Lord and believed that God would deliver him. Because he was a mighty man of valor, others who knew of his fight and communicated with him via social media, became mighty men and women of valor. As the eleven men of valor risked their lives to help David unite the kingdom and become King over all of Jerusalem, so Taurean's friends and social media acquaintances overcame insurmountable odds. They too developed a strong faith in God and broke through large numbers of health obstacles. They too demonstrated a boldness of determination in facing great danger, especially in battle. They too showed heroic courage and bravery in the face of adversity and communicated their successes on Facebook!

Remember earlier I stated that you can't judge a book by its cover, *"because the Lord seeth not as man seeth; for man looketh on the outward appearance, but the Lord looketh on the heart!"* Well, the other day, at 2:19 AM, early Tuesday morning, September the 5th... 2017, the death angel looked at the outer appearance of my son Taurean. It saw a weakened and fragile body. It saw the anguish in his eyes and the strain of pain on his face. So it proclaimed that it had won the battle. The Goliath called Cancer thought that it had finally accomplished its task. It thought that Taurean had lost the battle and that it now reigned victorious. They, the death angel and cancer, thought that my son had died, but this mighty man of valor fooled them again. He did what he's been doing over the last seven years. For at 2:20 AM his face changed. The anguish and pain of the battle against death and cancer left his face and a slight smile appeared on his lips. In my mind's eye and inner ear, I could see and hear my son saying: *"O Death, where is thy sting? O grave where is thy victory? For I am now ready to be offered and the time of my departure is at hand. I have fought a good fight, I have finished my course, I have kept the faith. Henceforth there is laid up for me a crown of righteousness, which the Lord, the righteous judge, shall give me at that day: and not to me only, but unto all them also that love his appearing."*[3]

---

[3] I Corinthians 15:55, 2 Timothy 4:6-7.

So death and cancer, what you meant for evil, God meant for good. You just don't know how many lives I've touched. You don't know how many warriors I've helped to train. You just don't know how many mighty men and women of valor that I've influenced and prepared to do battle with you.

See, all you see is this withered shell of a body on the outside, but on the inside I'm free. *"Eye hath not seen, nor ear heard, neither have entered into the heart of man, the things which God has prepared for them that love him."*[4]

Mr. Death and Mr. Cancer, where I am now you can't come, because the Bible says that *"there shall be no more death, neither sorrow, nor pain, nor crying, for the former things are passed away."*[5]

Mr. Death and Mr. Cancer, where I am, you can't come, because you both are creatures of the dark, and creatures of the dark love the darkness. My Bible taught me that there shall be no night here, and that I need no candle here, not even the light of the sun, for the Lord God now gives me the light.[6]

Mr. Death and Mr. Cancer, where I am now you can't come, because all you see is this outer shell of a tabernacle that I used to live in. My Bible taught me that

---

[4] 1 Corinthians 2:9.

[5] Revelation 21:4.

[6] Revelation 21:23.

when my earthy house of this tabernacle is dissolved, hallelujah, I have a building from God, a house not made with hands, eternal in the heavens.[7] My momma is here, and my grandparents are here, and a great crowd of witnesses are here.

And just in case you're wondering how I'm doing, just know that this mighty man of valor is doing fine. I can't complain!

God bless you!

---

[7] 2 Corinthians 5:1.

6

Eulogy for the Young Victims of the Sixteenth Street Baptist Church Bombing: Typescript

MARTIN LUTHER KING, JR.
EBENEZER BAPTIST CHURCH
ATLANTA, GA

At the time he delivered a version of this eulogy, Martin Luther King, Jr. (1929-1968), along with his father, co-pastored Ebenezer Baptist Church, Atlanta, GA. King received the B.A. from Morehouse College, the B.D. from Crozer Theological Seminary, and the Ph.D. from Boston University. The eulogy, as delivered, recorded, edited, and eventually published,[1] *is predicated upon but diverges*

---

[1] *A Call to conscience: The landmark speeches of Dr. Martin Luther King, Jr.*, ed. C. Carson/K. Shepard (New York/Boston: IPM/Warner Books, 2001), 95-99.

sharply from this typescript in the Martin Luther King, Jr. Center for Non-Violent Social Change archives. In the current presentation, I have endeavored to retain the typescript's peculiarities of grammar and punctuation and have added footnotes to explain some of the allusions and references. For permission to publish this typescript, I am grateful to the heirs to the estate of Martin Luther King Jr., c/o Writers House as agent for the proprietor, New York, NY.

FORWARD

The struggle over the segregation of Birmingham's business community and government culminated with the bombing of that city's Sixteenth Street Baptist Church. A campaign by several civil rights organizations, including Martin Luther King, Jr.'s Southern Christian Leadership Conference, ended during the spring of 1963 with some agreements to pursue desegregation. Some other bombings had occurred during the campaign, and photos of police using high-pressure water hoses and German shepherds had rallied national support for the protesters. During the demonstrations, the church had served as a staging area for several peaceful marches. This bombing, in contrast, garnered nationwide attention by killing four children.

More than fifty years later, classifying an incident of this sort as an example domestic terrorism would not be controversial. In 1963, in contrast, it might have been considered a direct reprisal. First, the attack was lodged against a church that had served as a staging area for some protest activities. Second, the timing on Youth Day served as a response to King's use of teenagers in his Birmingham protests. In any case, King was asked to preach a joint funeral for three of the four victims.

King's typescript refers to "a glorious march on the nation's Capitol." This event, the August 28, 1963 poor people's march on Washington, occurred as some measures of desegregation were being implemented in Birmingham. The march culminated with a speech that gave King unparalleled acclaim.[2] On September 15, 1963, less than three weeks later, a bomb placed under the front steps of the Sixteenth Street Baptist Church damaged the facility, injured a number of congregants, and killed four adolescent girls awaiting the church's annual Youth Day service.[3]

Several civil rights factions with varying opinions about violence participated in the march on Washington. King used *I have a dream* to plead with them to support his nonviolent approach. King used a dialectical outline to great effect. He began by acknowledging his listeners' cognitive dissonance, that is, by contrasting the possibilities created by the 1863 emancipation proclamation (thesis) with the conditions of continuing segregation and harassment prevalent in 1963 (antithesis).[4] A longer,

---

[2]I have a dream, *Call to conscience*, 81-87.

[3]Suzanne E. Smith, *To serve the living: Funeral directors and the African American way of death* (Cambridge/London: Harvard Univ., 2010), 154.

[4]I have a dream, *Call to conscience*, 81.

central section advocated the continuation of activism and warned the activists to conduct their struggle ethically and non-violently and not to distrust all Caucasians. When the listeners might return to their homes, they should not be overcome by desperation. This central section, the heart of the speech, took direct aim at those civil rights factions that were more permissive regarding the rhetoric of violence.

King's speech, like Pompey's nearly a century earlier, ended with a burst of visual and musical imagery. King's speech used a double refrain as its concluding synthesis. The sections beginning with "I have a dream..." depicted the behaviors King hoped might materialize. The impact of the final, repeated refrain, "Let freedom ring..." depended on the recollection and iconic photo of Marian Anderson's 1939 performance of the patriotic hymn, *My country, 'tis of thee,* also at the Lincoln Memorial.

The typescript followed in much the same vein as *I have a dream*. It began with a brief contrast of Sunday as a day of rest and worship (thesis) with the destruction and disorder of the fatal bombing (antithesis). After this introduction, King began to lay out his application of theodicy. He contrasted God's permissive will that allowed bombing and martyrdom with God's absolute will that the brutal system of segregation and its underlying philosophy be changed. As in *I have a dream*, he warned the activists to be more concerned about the system that encouraged murder than about the murderers themselves. Next, the typescript reached its synthesis with the assurance that "we shall overcome," a generalization of the previously expressed hope that the tragic bombing and its immediate aftermath might precipitate reconciliation. The typescript concluded by paraphrasing a line from *Hamlet* to commit the bodies to the earth.

In the typescript, King encouraged his prospective listeners to respond to the bombing by continuing to march and demonstrate. In other words, he proposed to maintain the movement's practice of non-violent, direct action, even in response to the escalation of hostilities that the bombing represented. The context does not indicate clearly whether King envisioned the resumption of non-violent protests in Birmingham or the initiation of such demonstrations in other theaters of operation. This section asserted directly that the bombing should not precipitate a more forceful, potentially violent, policy. When King modified the eulogy for delivery, he left out both the section on theodicy and that on the continuation of non-violent protest as the most appropriate response to the bombing.

The eulogy actually delivered was predicated on but differed substantially from the typescript. The sermon moved from a civil rights emphasis to a more pastoral perspective. It began with a reference to the quiet sanctuary and introduced the subjects of the eulogy with a theatrical metaphor.[5] At this stage King subordinated dialectic to direct transformation, emphasizing this process to a greater extent than he did in the typescript or in *I have a dream*. In the eulogy as delivered, King buttressed the

---

[5]Eulogy, *Call to conscience*, 95.

argument he made in the typescript that tragedy might catalyze positive social change. After some doctrinal items pertaining to a Christian perspective on death and the afterlife, he closed the sermon with the line from *Hamlet*, encompassing the entire work with an *inclusio*.[6]

King neither mentioned the victims by name nor discussed any of their unique characteristics in either version of the eulogy. In the typescript, he compared them to Medgar Evers and William Moore, both of whom had been assassinated earlier in 1963 for their civil rights activism. By foregoing individual description, King remained evenhanded in his treatment of the victims. In addition, he subordinated their individual differences to the experience of a violent death, which they shared with Evers and Moore, and expressed the hope that their deaths would contribute eventually to racial reconciliation.

The sermon composition process occurred within a compressed time frame. King was informed of the tragedy no earlier than Sunday September 15, 1963, and preached the funeral on Wednesday, September 18, 1963. Within a period of about 72 hours, he wrote the typescript, altered the sermon, and then delivered the eulogy as modified.

The typescript sheds some light on King's perspective immediately after *I have a dream* but leaves other questions unanswered. Emphasizing the pastoral role over that of civil right activist required some cognitive and emotional restructuring during the three days between the bombing and the funeral. The two roles, of course,

---

[6]Eulogy, *Call to conscience.*, 99.

represent different but complementary perspectives rather than mutually exclusive professional identities. The extent to which King's ministerial responsibilities may have facilitated this change in focus during the weeks between *I have a dream* and the bombing is uncertain. The eulogy as delivered dispensed with the section on theodicy but then dealt with bereavement issues more directly than did the typescript.

Both the typescript and the eulogy as delivered display characteristics of classical apology. In other words, they use different methods to defend King's philosophy of non-violence as appropriate and sufficient, even in light of the increased brutality that the bombing represented. Both addressed the possible perception that the murder of young children might require measures more extreme than non-violent protest. Both the typescript's explicit presentation of theodicy and the delivered eulogy's argument that righteous suffering might have redemptive consequences bolstered King's conclusion that non-violence remained the most appropriate path forward, even after the bombing.

Whether or not King believed there was a connection between the success of *I have a dream* and the behavior of the bombers is not known. Both the typescript and the eulogy as delivered clearly represent a struggle to derive a measure of positive impact from a tragedy. It would have been logical for King to consider the bombing a retaliatory response both to the success of his use of youthful protestors in marches initiated at the church and to that of his subsequent speech at the conclusion of the poor people's march on Washington. At this point, whether or not King subscribed to such logic and whether or not, for that reason, he may have felt some responsibility for the bombing, cannot be ascertained

One should take care neither to exaggerate nor to minimize the impact of King's eulogy on the subsequent course of the civil rights movement. Almost forty years after the event, Fred Shuttlesworth, a minister who had merged his own organization into King's Southern Christian Leadership Conference, implied that the eulogy did have an impact. He recalled that "the Klan bombing of the Sixteenth Street Baptist Church ... brought heartache and sorrow to [the victims'] families, gloom to Birmingham, and recognition of true brutality to the nation."[7] He wondered how those affected most profoundly might respond. "Would the grieving parents and friends of these four girls entertain thoughts of anger and blame, or would they accept their great loss as God's will?"[8] With the benefit of many years distance, he realized that King had delivered the eulogy in a situation in which his words might sway the listeners toward either retaliatory violence or continued non-violent, direct action.

Both the typescript and the eulogy as delivered reinforce Shuttlesworth's memory of King as a steadfast practitioner and proponent of non-violent, direct action. In both versions, King espoused non-violence unequivocally.

---

[7]Introduction to King, Eulogy, *Call to conscience*, 91.

[8]*Ibid.*

Immediately after the eulogy, the civil rights movement largely continued to follow King's model.

The fragmentation of the civil rights movement probably was inevitable, but the eulogy may have helped to forestall this process. King received a Nobel Peace Prize in 1964 for his accomplishments in 1963. He subsequently opposed the Vietnam War and focused his activism on economic disparities. By then, the Civil Rights Act and the Voting Rights Act had become the law of the land. Perhaps King's uncompromising insistence on a non-violent, direct response to the bombing encouraged the movement's various factions to continue cooperating in a manner that preserved their credibility until they won the legislative victories that represent the movement's high-water mark.

EDITOR

On last Sunday morning—the Lord's day, death came, destruction and horror came to this city. When the sun was shining, when souls of the church were worshipping God, when God's people were prepared for the music of the organ and the message of God's words. Suddenly loud and destructive blasts were heard and within minutes God's temple was rent assunder [sic] and when the smoke cleared and the noise closed, the bodies of innocent children were found crushed beneath the weight of crashing bombs. In Birmingham which we had believed to be a city redeemed, a crucifixion, had taken place. The three children, unoffending, innocent and beautiful, whose death we now observe, were the victims of this brutality which has echoed around the world. Today in the sacred services which commit them back to that eternity from which they came, we are constrained to ask, where was God in the midst of falling bombs?

Our tradition, our faith, our loyalty are taxed today as we gaze upon the caskets which hold the bodies of these three children. Some of us cannot understand why God will permit death and destruction to come to those who had done no man harm.

In order to understand what has happened, in order to maintain our sanity in the face of demonical [sic] insanity of the murderers who have taken these beautiful youngsters from our breasts, we must understand that God has a permissive will. God who is all powerful, sometimes allows things to happen because when he created man, he had to give man the right to exercise good and evil.

On the other hand, God has an obsolute [sic] positive will on this level. God ordains that things must happen only for good. He will not cooperate with evil.

God did not will that bombs should fall on the 16th Street Baptist Church or dictate the death of these three young girls but because God gave man his reign,[9] he had to allow the forces of evil to destroy a church and to take the lives of these dearly beloved. But God is the Supreme Court beyond which there is no appeal. And God has a

---

[9]Possibly a double entendre, both free rein and reign in the sense of human hegemony.

purpose and a will which will transform this tragic moment of our suffering into a magic eternity of redemption.

Not many weeks ago, this community—a community which had been domsed[10] as the worst segregated city in America, went through a period of trauma and turmoil out of which there emerged a mandate for the freedom and justice not only for the Negro people but for the people of this city and the nation. Out of this turbulence and travail a stupendous and magnificent revolution took place, culminating in a glorious march on the nation's Capitol. There is no doubt in the minds of some men that the Negro is on the high road to the Supreme highway of full democracy and first class citizenship. There has been a tremendous battle to win this victory.

In every battle for freedom there are martyrs whose lives are forfeited and whose sacrifices endorses [sic] the promise of liberty. These three girls whose bodies are encased in the caskets of death are such martyrs. They died as the result of the Holy Crusade of black men to be free—and because of the Holy Crusade of black men to be free the soul of all God's children regardless of race or color.

They were not civil rights leaders as the late mourned Medgar Evers, they were not crusaders of justice as the last[11] William Moore a Baltimore Postman who was

---

[10]Author's intention is uncertain (deemed? demonized?).

[11]A typographical error for "late." Moore was assassinated less than five months before the church bombing, during a solo march which he

gunned down as he sought to deliver the message of Democracy to the citadel of injustice. They were youngsters a tiny bit removed from baby food, and babies we are told are the latest news from heaven. So children are a glorious promise—and no one can tell what these children could have become—another Mary Bethune, another Daisy Bates, another Mahalia Jackson.

But they have become the most glorious that they could have become. They have become symbols of our crusade. They have given their lives to insure [sic] our liberty. They did not do this deliberately. They did it because something strange, something incomprehensible to man is re-enacted in God's will and they are home today with God.

Their death in the rubble of a bombed church represents murder. Not only their murder but the murder of all humanity. They symbolize our faith—they have something to say to us in their death. They say to leaders and to men and to politicians and to people that we must substitute courage for caution. They say to mankind that we must condemn not only the bitterness of bad people but the silence of good people.[12] Their deaths say that when the 16th Street Baptist Church was assailed by bombs the institutions of our land, of our world were assailed.

---

had intended to conclude by delivering a letter supportive of civil rights to Mississippi's governor. Evers, likewise, was assassinated in 1963.

[12]King elaborated this theme in a memorable way during the early portion of the eulogy that he actually delivered.

We are not concerned today about who murdered these children who lie here, the martyred heroines of our struggle, we are concerned about the system, the way of life, the philosophy which produces the murderer. We say, "Father, forgive them for they know not what they do." But we believe when all of the battles are through that the day will come when we will change that system, alter that way of life, transform that philosophy and we shall not sit and mourn and grieve and be docile. We shall march and we shall demonstrate and we shall present our living bodies as witness to the cause for which these beautiful young and lifeless bodies have been given. We shall overcome[13] because these children who belong to that pledge of humanity—that Christ shall lead them[14]—has showed [sic] us the way.

> The roar of the beast is loud in the land,
> And the beast has struck
> But he's got the wild beast in his hand.
> And the avenging angel is on the wing
> And the wind is blowing in from the sea.[15]

---

[13] An allusion to a spiritual, with tune derived from Sicilian Mariners, which became the anthem of the civil rights movement.

[14] In the eulogy actually delivered, this passage became "a little child shall lead them" (Isaiah 11:6). The literary context of the eulogy suggests that King had in mind the entire passage, which paired predatory with domesticated animals, all led by a child, as a metaphor for the reconciliation which he hoped might follow this tragedy.

[15] Allusion is uncertain but possibly a free application of Revelation 13.

Three souls have been released by the striking beast. Weep not. Know the hour is dark and the way is hard; the beast will not escape from the hand of God. They died within the sacred walls of the church after discussing a principle as eternal as love.[16]

Shakespeare had Horatio utter some beautiful words over the dead body of Hamlet. I paraphrase these words today as I stand over the last remains of these lovely girls. "Good night, sweet princesses. May the flight of angels take thee to thy eternal rest."[17]

---

[16] King elaborated this theme during the latter portion of the eulogy actually delivered.

[17] 5:2:344-345.

7

In Remembrance:
Saying Good-bye and Honoring a Legacy

NICOLE DANIELLE MCDONALD
SENTARA HOSPICE
HAMPTON, VA

Both the Jewish and the Christian scriptural canons include recycled materials. A comparison of the Samuel-Kings narrative to the Chronicler's account in the Jewish literature or a consideration of the synoptic problem in the Christian canon illustrates this point. Likewise, Colossians updates and summarizes some materials derived from the undisputed Pauline epistles.

Clergy are as prone to recycling as were those precursors who compiled the two scriptural anthologies. I myself have reworked several sermons by emphasizing different perspectives or by adding new or removing old components for various audiences or altered situations.

In this set of three eulogies, the minister, a hospice chaplain, presents three variants of the same sermon. In each case, she uses the sermon to reinforce the fact that a death constitutes an irreversible loss. Since a hospice is a medical setting rather than a church, the chaplain serves families with a variety of religious beliefs and experiences. The patients have in common only the facts that their physicians have predicted, in writing, that they will die within six months and that they have responded to this diagnosis and prognosis by choosing palliative care rather than aggressive treatment.

These eulogies exemplify an approach to sermon preparation when circumstances limit the minister's ability to learn about the deceased. In the first case, the patient spent only two days on the hospice service. However, a two-hour conversation with the decedent's wife facilitated funeral planning. In the other cases, brief conversations with the decedents' relatives suggested adaptations of the first sermon. All three eulogies emphasized the process of saying good-bye and the importance to the survivors of incorporating remembrance rituals into their lifestyles.

EUCHARISTIC TEXTS: AN OVERVIEW

McDonald's recycling process begins with the selection of a recycled text. Early Christian literature includes four treatments of the last supper or rituals derived from it. The synoptic treatment occurs in three versions, and McDonald uses the Lucan version as the text for all three of her eulogies. Thus, we begin by examining the available texts to elucidate the advantages that McDonald's selection provided for her eulogies.

Didache 9-10 restricts participation in the Eucharist to baptized believers. This passage specifies three prayers, first over the cup, next over the broken bread, and, finally, a general prayer of thanksgiving. The order of the elements (cup, then bread) differs from that in the other traditions but bears some affinity to the longer Lucan text in McDonald's preferred translation. The prayers emphasize a desire for Christian unification more than they do an interest in events either from Jesus' life or from Jewish antecedents. More importantly, the prayer over the bread and the concluding prayer of thanksgiving are compatible with the oaths of Luke 22:16-18.

In 1 Corinthians 11:17-26, Paul criticizes the manner in which that fellowship perpetuated the Lord's Supper tradition that Paul claimed to have received and passed down. In this tradition, both the blessed and broken bread and the wine after supper were consumed in the Lord's memory. The ritual, as a whole, commemorated the Lord's death until he should come. Paul's Lord's Supper apparently held a function similar to those of the memorial meals common among burial societies of that era. More importantly to the relationship of the Eucharistic traditions, Paul specified that the relevant cup followed the meal.

The fourth gospel's bread of life discourse (6:30-51) constitutes a *midrash* (meditation) on both the exodus manna account and the last supper tradition of the bread and wine. It is not associated closely with Passover. Like much of the fourth gospel, it illustrates a pattern of finding contemporaneous Judaism simultaneously attractive and repulsive.[1] As in Paul's tradition, the metaphorical consumption of Jesus' blood would be more amenable to certain types of Gentile converts than to Jewish proselytes.

Finally, we come to the synoptic tradition. Mark 14:1-25 characterizes this last supper explicitly as a component of a Passover (unleavened bread) *seder* that Jesus observed with his closest followers. Both Luke and Matthew include the Marcan account, which they then augment with materials from their unique traditions.

The Lucan narrative in its longer form, preserved primarily in the western text family, includes a cup before and another cup after the bread.[2] The first cup is followed by the oath with which the Marcan account concludes, while the second incorporates the interpretation of the single cup in Mark 14:24.

Last supper narratives typically include bread and cup in that order, each typically accompanied by words of institution. The longer version of the Lucan narrative is unique in describing a last supper which included a cup, the

---

[1] Charles Kingsley Barrett, *The Gospel of John and Judaism*, tr. D. M. Smith (Philadelphia: Fortress, 1975).

[2] The western text family (Vaticanus, *et al*) generally has a longer text than does the Alexandrian family. In accordance with the usual canons of textual criticism, the shorter readings typically are considered more likely early or authentic. In the case of Luke, there is some tendency to favor some of the longer, western readings which, consequently, are called the western non-interpolations.

breaking of bread, and another cup after the bread. Nevertheless, the materials reviewed above indicate that the two-cup tradition antedates the third gospel. The Didache places the cup before the bread, the opposite of the usual order, and includes prayers for unity which are compatible with the Lucan narrative's oaths concerning the kingdom of God. Paul specifies that the relevant cup and related words of institution occurred after supper. Thus, he may have presumed the presence of a first cup which was not relevant to the observance he described, since the oath associated with that cup was comparable in some sense to his subsequent elaboration of the ritual's role as a memorial observance. We conclude that the Pauline and the Didache accounts reflect an awareness of a two-cup tradition within their prehistory. The oath over the first cup in the extant two-cup tradition mirrors the function of the final cup of restoration in some contemporary, four-cup Passover *seders*. For Mark, who used the oath as a conclusion, and Paul, who replaced the oath with a similar conclusion more comprehensible to his Gentile converts, the first cup was superfluous. Thus, we make no judgement as to whether or not the Lucan version attached this oath to the cup with which it most likely would have been associated in an earlier Jewish milieu.

McDonald uses a translation of the Lucan narrative that assumes the priority of the longer, western text. Her sermonic text (Luke 22:14-20, NIV) includes the two-cup tradition in its entirety. During the eulogies, she passes over the first cup (pun intended) and focuses on the bread and the second cup. I would surmise that her decision is grounded in the following two factors. First, particularly in the first (Miles Chopping) eulogy, she is fully engaged in the contemporary Christian custom of observing the Lord's Supper with only one cup of grape juice or wine. Habit has taken over. More importantly, the first cup in the Lucan narrative, much like the cup of restoration in a *seder*, is associated solely with an oath not to drink of the fruit of the vine until the kingdom of God should arrive (22:18). This association renders the first cup unimportant in light of her focus on leave-taking followed by rituals of remembrance.

EDITOR

The three eulogies below are variants of the same theme. The first decedent spent only two days in hospice care. McDonald reported that, during that period, she had a conversation of about two hours with his wife. This conversation guided her into the development of a full-fledged eulogy for a retired veteran who was very religious and a devoted family man. As noted in the eulogy itself, the sermon led directly to the Lord's Supper. Two of the names have been changed; the first decedent, whose funeral was held on May 17, 2015, is here called Miles Chopping.

SERMONIC TEXT: THE LAST SUPPER
Luke 22:14-20, New International Version

> [14]When the hour came, Jesus and his apostles reclined at the table. [15]And he said to them, "I have eagerly desired

to eat this Passover with you before I suffer. [16]For I tell you, I will not eat it again until it finds fulfillment in the kingdom of God." [17]After taking the cup, he gave thanks and said, "Take this and divide it among you. [18]For I tell you I will not drink again of the fruit of the vine until the kingdom of God comes." [19]And he took bread, gave thanks and broke it, and gave it to them, saying, "This is my body given for you; do this in remembrance of me." [20]In the same way, after the supper he took the cup, saying, "This cup is the new covenant in my blood, which is poured out for you."

It's hard to say goodbye to those we love. And, is there such a thing as a GOOD-BYE when speaking to those we love dearly, persons that we would like to be with forever? Furthermore, as we leave our loved ones, I suspect there are more significant things we would say, rather than just goodbye, if we knew our time was drawing near.

In the text this afternoon, Jesus has the monumental task of saying goodbye to his beloved disciples, knowing that the time had come for the fulfillment of scripture, when he would be crucified on the cross. He gathered the disciples in the upper room to celebrate the Passover, as was customary during this period. But this time, the celebration was different. Unbeknownst to the disciples, this would be the Last Supper, the last Passover Celebration with Jesus here on earth, the last meal they would ever share with their companion and friend. But Jesus knew this was the Last Supper. He knew that this was his opportunity to say goodbye. Therefore, he sets a precedent for the perfect goodbye.

The first thing that Jesus shows us is that goodbyes are to celebrate life. In verse 15, Jesus says, "I have eagerly desired to eat this Passover with you before I suffer." It is no coincidence that Jesus plans the goodbye during the Passover meal. If we remember from the Old Testament, Passover comes the tenth plague, where the Lord decided to the kill the firstborn son in all of Egypt. You remember the story, Moses said to Pharaoh, "Let my people go," and the Lord hardened Pharaoh's heart. In order for the firstborn son to be spared, the Israelites placed the blood of the lamb on their doors, so that the death angel would *PASS OVER* their house. After the death of the first born sons, Pharaoh relented and set the Israelites free. The Passover ritual not only celebrates the Israelites' freedom from slavery, but it also celebrates the lives that were spared, the firstborn sons.

So as we say goodbye to Miles Chopping, let us celebrate his life and all the things that make him uniquely Miles. The Lord gave him to us for 64 years. He lived a full life traveling the world, serving our country, enjoying the simple things in life – nature, the outdoors, friends, family, love and laughter. Teach us to number our days[3] so that we, too, can live life to the fullest, loving one another unconditionally and spending quality time with those we love.

---

[3] C.f., Psalm 39:4, 90:12.

Since Miles was a retired military veteran, we can honestly say that the death angel passed over him in times of war as he served this country with distinction. Though we wish the death angel had passed over him once again, we can still celebrate his life by doing what Jesus did because a perfect goodbye is one that celebrates life by eating, drinking, and enjoying our family and friends.

The second thing that Jesus shows us is that goodbyes are to cherish love. We cherish love by telling our love stories. In verse 20, Jesus tells the love story of the gospel. He says, "This cup is the new covenant in my blood, which is poured out for you." Here Jesus alludes to his blood being poured out on the cross on Calvary for the forgiveness of our sins. Is this not the ultimate love story, a story of unconditional, sacrificial love, representative of the covenant between us and our Savior? "God so loved the world that he gave his only begotten son, that whosoever believes in him shall not perish, but have eternal life" (John 3:16, KJV). That's love.

A perfect goodbye cherishes love by sharing our love stories, the story of a man who fell in love the first time he laid eyes on his beautiful bride-to-be, neither of whom were looking for love, but love found them anyway. Miles was so smitten that he persistently asked Barbara out until she finally said yes. Miles' romantic side came through when he sent love notes through the fax machine. Tell the love story that highlights the great times before Miles' illness, in the garage working on cars, Miles being a prankster, the quality time with family and friends in the back yard on the grill by the pool. Towards the end of Miles' illness, he could not communicate verbally and had difficulty communicating with his eyes. But one thing that his eyes always communicated was his love for his wife, his family, and his love for all of his nurses who cared for him with such compassion. Tell the love story that was built on the covenant that was made, for better or for worse, until death do us part, that unconditional, sacrificial love that loved Miles through his illness all the way to eternal life. Tell the story because that's how we cherish our love.

The last thing that Jesus shows us about goodbyes is that a perfect goodbye continues the legacy. In verse 19 Jesus says, "This is my body given for you; do this in remembrance of me." We celebrate the Last Supper in remembrance of Christ's unconditional love for us through his crucifixion on the cross for the redemption of our sins. Continue the legacy of Christ through our unconditional love for one another on earth. Our love draws people to us, as the love of Christ draws us to the Lord. Share this love with one another freely. Do this in remembrance of Christ.

In remembrance of Miles, do rituals that honor his legacy. How are the grandchildren going to know Miles, if we don't do rituals in remembrance of him? As time goes on, don't be afraid to talk about Miles, share a laugh or two, go through the photo albums with the grandkids. Keep his memory alive. Continue the legacy of Miles Chopping by coming together as family and friends, eating, drinking, loving and laughing not only because Miles would want you to do this, but because that is the precedent set by Jesus Christ.

In closing, as I raise this glass and a piece of bread as elements of communion, the sacrament of the church that is modeled in the text this afternoon in Luke 22, let us continue to be mindful of the precedent of Jesus Christ. That on the night that Jesus was betrayed he took bread; and when He had given thanks, He broke it and said, "Take, eat this is my body which is broken for you, do this in remembrance of me. And in the same manner, He also took the cup saying, "This cup is the new covenant in my blood. Drink it, in remembrance of me. This represents the blood of our Lord Jesus Christ through which He ensured the forgiveness of our sins. For as often as we eat this bread and drink this cup, we proclaim the Lord's death 'til He comes again.

Because of Miles' water baptism into the Kingdom of God, today, we celebrate Miles' life, cherish his love, and continue his legacy, believing in the promise of eternal life with our Lord and Savior Jesus Christ. Believe in the Lord Jesus and his promises. You will be reunited with Miles and Jesus one day!" God bless you. Amen.

The second eulogy, derived from the first, was delivered at the funeral of a decedent whose family requested remarks that were "short and sweet." The wife was a faithful churchgoer. Charlie Freeman Billups, Sr., in contrast, was a devoted family man but did not attend church. He was memorialized on February 16, 2019, and his widow subsequently requested that his actual name be used in this anthology.

I can remember growing up as a child and visiting my Grandmother's house. She had that iconic picture in her living room of Jesus and the disciples sitting at that long table experiencing the Last Supper. In church I learned that the picture was Jesus sharing one last meal with his disciples before the fulfillment of scripture. But now as a young woman who has experienced the ups and downs of life, joys and sorrows, and yes, love and loss, I realize that it is much more than just a last meal. It was Jesus' last chance to enjoy one more fellowship with his friends that he had journeyed with throughout his 3 years in ministry. It was Jesus' opportunity to say goodbye to his beloved friends who had become his family.

In the narrative of the Last Supper, Jesus models how we can say goodbye to those we love. The first thing that we learn is that a GOOD-bye is to celebrate life. Jesus and the disciples are sitting around the table eating a meal. In the African American tradition, meals bring us together. Meals provide comfort. Meals are how we celebrate. After graduations, what did you do? You went out to eat. For birthdays, what did you do? You had the cook-out in the backyard celebrating life. On Sundays after church, you gathered at the table as a family for love and laughter to talk about life or maybe just to reflect on the week or maybe just to talk about preacher's hour-long sermon.

So, as you prepare your hearts for a GOOD-bye, you too can reflect on the special meals you've shared with Mr. Billups; the Christmas dinners, the Thanksgiving feasts, the weddings, and even the meals that were special because of his presence, as a father, a husband, an uncle, and a friend. Celebrate his life by continuing to gather together for special meals.

The second thing we learn is that a GOOD-bye is to cherish love. Jesus shared the Last Supper with his disciples as an act of the cherished love that was shared between them after 3 long years of ministry; healing the sick, casting out demons, feeding the multitude, preaching on mountains, in homes, and by the seashore. If you would allow me to use my sanctified imagination, I believe that Jesus and the disciples were not just sharing a meal, but they were sharing stories of their 3 year journey. You know how we do. "Remember when we were on the boat scared to death. We didn't know what to do. Jesus was sleeping in the bow. We woke him up and he just said, "Peace, be still" (Mark 4:39). Man that was an awesome day. Jesus spoke to the wind and it ceased. What about that time when all those people were hungry and we only had a little boy's lunch? Somehow Jesus fed all those people and had some to spare.

We cherish love by sharing our love stories. Yvonne, share the love story of your marriage with Charlie that lasted over 52 years. Children, share your love story of your father who gave unconditional love. Brothers and sisters share your childhood memories of growing up with Charlie because THAT IS LOVE.

The last thing that Jesus shows us is that a GOOD-bye continues the legacy. Jesus says, "Do this in remembrance of me." We celebrate the Last Supper in remembrance of Christ's unconditional love for us. Continue the legacy of Christ through our unconditional love for one another on earth.

In remembrance of Charlie, do rituals that honor his legacy. Continue the legacy of Mr. Billups by taking a walk in a garden. He loved the outdoors and experiencing nature. Consider planting a flower in his honor. But most of all, do something that brings you joy in honor of your experiences with him. Maybe he taught you how to drive. So, teaching someone else how to drive may be a way to honor your experiences with Mr. Billups. Maybe he was that person that always shared a kind word with you. In honor of his legacy, you share kind words with others.

Another way that you may continue the legacy of Mr. Billups is by listening to music. He was a lover of music, even becoming a disc jockey for events across Hampton Roads. I would imagine that he was most proud and honored to share his love of music at family events. Music has a way of bringing people together, making people smile, and giving people joy. So, while you're enjoying that special meal and sharing your love stories, why not play a little music, and get on that dance floor in honor of Charlie Billups. This is how you experience a GOOD-bye.

Finally, the third variant was delivered on June 30, 2019 for a decedent whose family requested something short. The family informed McDonald that the decedent, here called Larry Jones, did not attend church and did not do much of anything.

I can remember growing up as a child and visiting my Grandmother's house. She had that iconic picture in her living room of Jesus and the disciples sitting at that long table experiencing the Last Supper. In church I learned that the picture was Jesus sharing one last meal with his disciples before the fulfillment of scripture. But now as a young woman who has experienced the ups and downs of life, joys and sorrows, and yes, loves and lost, I realize that it is much more than just a last meal. It was Jesus' last chance to enjoy one more fellowship with his friends that he had journeyed with throughout his 3 years in ministry. It was Jesus' opportunity to say goodbye to his beloved friends who had become his family.

In the narrative of the Last Supper, Jesus models how we can say goodbye to those we love. The first thing that we learn is that a GOOD-bye is to celebrate life. Jesus and the disciples are sitting around the table eating a meal. In the African American tradition, meals bring us together. Meals provide comfort. Meals are how we celebrate. After graduations, what did you do? You went out to eat. For birthdays, what did you do? You had the cook-out in the backyard celebrating life. On Sunday's after church, you gathered at the table as a family for love and laughter to talk about life or maybe just to reflect on the week or maybe just to talk about preacher's hour-long sermon.

So, as you prepare your hearts for a GOOD-bye, you too can reflect on the special meals you've shared with Mr. Jones; the Christmas dinners, the Thanksgiving feasts, and even the meals that were special because of his presence, as a brother, an uncle, and a friend. Celebrate life by continuing to gather together for special meals.

The second thing we learn is that a GOOD-bye is to cherish love. Jesus shared the Last Supper with his disciples as an act of the cherished love that was shared between them after 3 long years of ministry; healing the sick, casting out demons, feeding the multitude, preaching on mountains, in homes, and by the seashore. If you would allow me to use my sanctified imagination, I believe that Jesus and the disciples were not just sharing a meal, but they were sharing stories of their 3 year journey. You know how we do. "Remember when we were on the boat scared to death. We didn't know what to do. Jesus was sleeping in the bow. We woke him up and he just said, "Peace, be still" (Mark 4:39). Man that was an awesome day. Jesus spoke to the wind and it ceased. What about that time when all those people were hungry and we only had a little boy's lunch? Somehow Jesus fed all those people and had some to spare. Jesus, we have seen you do some miraculous things over the years. Jesus, I know we don't always get it. Do you remember when we were arguing about who is the greatest? And, when we couldn't cast out that demon? We know we haven't always gotten things right."

Our love stories tell the ups and downs of life, the times when we've gotten it right and the times when we've missed the mark. Both successes and failures are a part of life. We cherish love by sharing the complex nature of life. Tell the truth about our complicated love. There is no shame in truth telling. We honor our love by sharing the truth about our love stories.

Brothers and sisters share your childhood memories of growing up with Larry because THAT IS LOVE. Nieces and nephews, share your love story about Uncle Larry. We keep love alive by speaking his name, Larry Jones. Share his story because that is how we say good-bye.

The last thing that Jesus shows us is that a GOOD-bye continues the legacy. Jesus says, "Do this in remembrance of me." We celebrate the Last Supper in remembrance of Christ's unconditional love for us. Continue the legacy of Christ through our unconditional love for one another on earth. As we say goodbye to Larry Jones this afternoon, consider how you might honor his legacy in the name of Jesus the Christ.

To honor someone's legacy can be quite simple. Once, I had a family who planted a tree in honor of their mother who was an avid gardener. Another time, I had a daughter tell me that every time she sees a cardinal, she smiles because that was her mother's favorite bird. The comfort of the cardinal honors her mother's legacy.

Do something in remembrance of Larry Jones! He was not a perfect man and neither are we. Christ died on the cross for all of our sins, mine, yours, and Larry's too. As we say goodbye to Larry Jones, let us celebrate life, cherish love, and continue the legacy. Amen.

8

Eulogy for the Honorable Reverend Clementa Pinckney

BARACK HUSSEIN OBAMA, II
EMANUEL AFRICAN METHODIST EPISCOPAL CHURCH
CHARLESTON, SC

Barack Obama was trained not as a minister but as an attorney. His skill as an orator enabled him to climb into the political elite rapidly. He served as an Illinois state senator for seven years and then as one of that state's U.S. senators for three years. He delivered the eulogy for Clementa Pinckney during the latter portion of his second term as U.S. president. This sermon is presented, courtesy of the U.S. National Archives and Records Administration's Barack Obama Presidential Library.

FORWARD

On June 17, 2015, Dylan Roof, a young Caucasian male, entered Charleston's Emanuel African Methodist Episcopal Church and shot to death nine individuals who were participating in a Bible study.[1] Roof subsequently admitted that he hoped to ignite a race war. In addition, he was found to be the owner of a white supremacist website.[2]

One of Roof's casualties was Clementa Carlos Pinckney, the church's pastor who served concurrently as a state senator. The shooting garnered nationwide attention, reigniting debates about race relations and the advantages and drawbacks of firearms control policies.

The unexpected, violent deaths of nine members of the same church created an immediate need for funeral services and pastoral care. Since one of the nine decedents was the pastor, the shooting also vacated the position primarily responsible for meeting those needs. The congregation was large. Without being directly familiar with the situation, I presume some level of vicarious traumatization among the surviving parishioners. Thus, the ability of the church to discharge its pastoral responsibilities was not immediately evident in the aftermath of the shooting.

Beyond the church walls, the shooting opened some undesirable possibilities regarding race relations throughout

---

[1] We identify Roof here as the shooter, without equivocation, since he was convicted of federal hate crimes and pled guilty to state murder charges in connection with the incident.

[2] https://en.wikipedia.org/wiki/Dylann_Roof (accessed 08/11/2019).

the nation. Would Roof succeed in igniting a race war? Alternatively, would African Americans and Caucasians retreat further into insular communities and thus exacerbate the nation's economic and racial polarization?

In short, the Emanuel AME shooting required a decisive, public response which the congregation and the denomination probably were not well equipped to provide. Among the Wesleyan denominations, clergy and laity have differing levels and types of authority, and the pastoral position had been vacated without warning. On the one hand, the congregation needed an opportunity to express its anger and grief. On the other hand, public expressions of these emotions needed to be kept under some level of control to prevent behaviors that might exacerbate the situation, not only in the church but nationwide. In short, the shooting required a response that was both pastoral and political. The circumstances dictated that leadership for this response would come from outside of the congregation, most likely from somebody with public recognition based on both political and religious factors.

Owing to his political stature, Barack Obama was a logical choice for the public role. However, he carried a polyvalent mixture of symbolism. Obama is a biracial individual who identifies himself, in accordance with his physical appearance, as a light-skinned African American. At the time, he was the entire nation's public face, having served more than six years as president. Among political progressives, his ascent to the nation's highest elected office represented an African American's achievement of the highest political aspiration possible in our nation's federal system. Among others, however, it represented a most devastating political setback. For white supremacists, Obama was an African American holding the high office previously occupied only by Caucasian males. To add insult to injury, he also was a biracial individual, the product of miscegenation. Diverse perspectives regarding the symbolism inherent in Obama's identity contributed to the ongoing polarization of American politics.

As head of state, Obama was already under some pressure to manage the incident's nationwide political fallout. The applicable article of the Constitution (2:2) pertains not to domestic issues but to the president's role in managing the military and conducting war. Nevertheless, there was some expectation that the president would take charge in the midst of crisis and keep the situation from spiraling out of control. In the absence of a pastor, Obama was particularly well positioned to lead the church in mourning its dead and to articulate a nationally relevant vision of race relations in the tragedy's aftermath, for better or for worse.

The history of Emanuel AME Church included several factors that might have turned the congregation and the building into high-value, symbolic targets for a white supremacist. Denmark Vesey, one of the congregation's founders, was convicted in a less-than-transparent trial of fomenting rebellion and was hanged. The 2015 shooting occurred the day after the anniversary of the discovery of Vesey's supposedly planned rebellion. The congregation met surreptitiously after the Caucasian governing class responded to Virginia's Nat Turner rebellion by closing the church. During Reconstruction, the wooden building that preceded the current structure was designed by architect Robert Vesey, Denmark Vesey's son. In 1962, Martin Luther King, Jr., whose work appears elsewhere in this volume, was a guest speaker. In 1969, his widow, Coretta Scott King, led a march that ended at the church with the arrest of a large number of protesters. By holding pastoral and political offices simultaneously, Pinckney followed the tradition established by some of his predecessors.

Obama's eulogy used a two-pronged strategy to manage the church's inherent symbolic factors. First, it reframed the church's history and its symbolic importance in positive terms with which a white supremacist would disagree. Second, it took aim at the publicly funded display of a southern symbol, the battle flag of the Army of Northern Virginia, over a Confederate monument near the state capitol.[3] Obama noted the polyvalent nature of the flag's symbolism, with the flag representing ancestral pride to some South Carolina residents but symbolizing systemic oppression and subjugation for others.

---

[3]The shooting provided an impetus for the July 10, 2015 removal of the flag to a Confederate museum. Two-thirds of each legislative chamber approved the removal, the Senate easily but the House only after contentious debate. Law enforcement investigated death threats to legislators on both sides. (https://www.theguardian.com/us-news/2015/jul/10/confederate-flag-south-carolina-statehouse [accessed August 11, 2019]).

The earliest audiences of Hebrews almost certainly construed Obama's text, (11:13) in terms of a platonistic distinction between the earthly and the heavenly realms. For Obama's purposes, in contrast, the text facilitated the questioning of present realities. The relegation of many African American youth to dilapidated schools, an overzealous criminal justice system, limited job prospects, and poverty came under the microscope, as did more subtle forms of discrimination. Specific proposals for reform, however, awaited a different circumstance. Thus, for Obama, the text suggested the hope for a contrast between present and future conditions in the mundane reality.

An elaboration of the doctrine of grace through faith provided a rationale for the questioning of the present situation. The paraphrase of a well-known passage from Paul's most famous epistle (Rom. 5:1-5) and the first verse of an equally famous hymn by John Newton framed this section. For Obama, the American emphasis on equality was consistent with Paul's argument that divine grace is a free gift that the recipient neither earns nor merits. This observation constitutes the foundation of Obama's exhortation to undertake a critical examination of economic and racial disparities.

EDITOR

Giving all praise and honor to God. (*Applause.*) The Bible calls us to hope, to persevere, and have faith in things not seen.

"They were still living by faith when they died," scripture tells us. "They did not receive the things promised; they only saw them and welcomed them from a distance, admitting that they were foreigners and strangers on Earth."[4]

We are here today to remember a man of God who lived by faith. A man who believed in things not seen. A man who believed there were better days ahead, off in the distance. A man of service who persevered, knowing full well he would not receive all those things he was promised, because he believed his efforts would deliver a better life for those who followed.

To Jennifer, his beloved wife; to Eliana and Malana, his beautiful, wonderful daughters; to the Mother Emanuel family and the people of Charleston, the people of South Carolina:

I cannot claim to have the good fortune to know Reverend Pinckney well. But I did have the pleasure of knowing him and meeting him here in South Carolina, back when we were both a little bit younger. (*Laughter.*) Back when I didn't have visible gray hair. (*Laughter.*) The first thing I noticed was his graciousness, his smile, his reassuring baritone, his deceptive sense of humor—all qualities that helped him wear so effortlessly a heavy burden of expectation.

Friends of his remarked this week that when Clementa Pinckney entered a room, it was like the future arrived; that even from a young age, folks knew he was

---

[4]Hebrews 11:13 (New International Version).

special. Anointed. He was the progeny of a long line of the faithful—a family of preachers who spread God's word, a family of protesters who sowed change to expand voting rights and desegregate the south. Clem heard their instruction, and he did not forsake their teaching.

He was in the pulpit by 13, pastor by 18, public servant by 23. He did not exhibit any of the cockiness of youth, nor youth's insecurities; instead, he set an example worthy of his position, wise beyond his years, in his speech, in his conduct, in his love, faith, and purity.

As a senator, he represented a sprawling swath of the low country, a place that has long been one of the most neglected in America. A place still wracked by poverty and inadequate schools; a place where children can still go hungry and the sick can go without treatment. A place that needed somebody like Clem. (*Applause*.)

His position in the minority party meant the odds of winning more resources for his constituents were often long. His calls for greater equity were too often unheeded; the votes he cast were sometimes lonely. But he never gave up. He stayed true to his convictions. He would not grow discouraged. After a full day at the capitol, he'd climb into his car and head to the church to draw sustenance from his family, from his ministry, from the community that loved and needed him. There he would fortify his faith and imagine what might be.

Reverend Pinckney embodied a politics that was neither mean nor small. He conducted himself quietly and kindly and diligently. He encouraged progress not by pushing his ideas alone but by seeking out your ideas, partnering with you to make things happen. He was full of empathy and fellow feeling, able to walk in somebody else's shoes and see through their eyes. No wonder one of his senate colleagues remembered Senator Pinckney as "the most gentle of the 46 of us—the best of the 46 of us."

Clem was often asked why he chose to be a pastor and a public servant. But the person who asked probably didn't know the history of the AME church. (*Applause*.) As our brothers and sisters in the AME church know, we don't make those distinctions. "Our calling," Clem once said, "is not just within the walls of the congregation but, ..., the life and community in which our congregation resides." (*Applause*.)

He embodied the idea that our Christian faith demands deeds and not just words; that the "sweet hour of prayer" actually lasts the whole week long—(*applause*)— that to put our faith in action is more than individual salvation, it's about our collective salvation; that to feed the hungry and clothe the naked and house the homeless is not just a call for isolated charity but the imperative of a just society.

What a good man. Sometimes I think that's the best thing to hope for when you're eulogized—after all the words and recitations and resumes are read, to just say someone was a good man. (*Yeah. Applause*.)

You don't have to be of high station to be a good man. Preacher by 13, pastor by 18, public servant by 23. What a life Clementa Pinckney lived. What an example he set. What a model for his faith. And then to lose him at 41—slain in his sanctuary with eight wonderful members of his flock, each at different stages in life but bound together by a common commitment to God.

Cynthia Hurd, Susie Jackson, Ethel Lance. DePayne Middleton-Doctor, Tzwanza Sanders, Daniel L. Simmons, Sharonda Coleman-Singleton, Myra Thompson. Good people. Decent people. God-fearing people. (*Applause.*) People so full of life and so full of kindness. People who ran the race, who persevered. People of great faith.

To the families of the fallen, the nation shares in your grief. Our pain cuts that much deeper because it happened in a church. The church is and always has been the center of African-American life—(*applause*)—a place to call our own in a too often hostile world, a sanctuary from so many hardships.

Over the course of centuries, black churches served as "hush harbors" where slaves could worship in safety; praise houses where their free descendants could gather and shout hallelujah—(*applause*)—rest stops for the weary along the underground railroad; bunkers for the foot soldiers of the civil rights movement. They have been, and continue to be, community centers where we organize for jobs and justice; places of scholarship and network; places where children are loved and fed and kept out of harm's way, and told that they are beautiful and smart—(*applause*)—and taught that they matter. (*Applause.*) That's what happens in church.

That's what the black church means. Our beating heart. The place where our dignity as a people is inviolate. When there's no better example of this tradition than Mother Emanuel—(*applause*)—a church built by blacks seeking liberty, burned to the ground because its founder sought to end slavery, only to rise up again, a phoenix from the ashes. (*Applause.*)

When there were laws banning all-black church gatherings, services happened here anyway, in defiance of unjust laws. When there was a righteous movement to dismantle Jim Crow, Dr. Martin Luther King, Jr. preached from its pulpit, and marches began from its steps. A sacred place, this church. Not just for blacks, not just for Christians, but for every American who cares about the steady expansion—(*applause*)—of human rights and human dignity in this country; a foundation stone for liberty and justice for all. That's what the church meant. (*Applause.*)

We do not know whether the killer of Reverend Pinckney and eight others knew all of this history. But he surely sensed the meaning of his violent act. It was an act that drew on a long history of bombs and arson and shots fired at churches, not random, but as a means of control, a way to terrorize and oppress. (*Applause.*) An act that he imagined would incite fear and recrimination, violence and suspicion. An act that he presumed would deepen divisions that trace back to our nation's original sin.

Oh, but God works in mysterious ways. (A*pplause*). God has different ideas. (*Applause.*)

He didn't know he was being used by God. (*Applause.*) Blinded by hatred, the alleged killer could not see the grace surrounding Reverend Pinckney and that Bible study group—the light of love that shone as they opened the church doors and invited a stranger to join in their prayer circle. The alleged killer could have never anticipated the way the families of the fallen would respond when they saw him in court—in the midst of unspeakable grief, with words of forgiveness. He couldn't imagine that. (*Yeah. Applause.*)

The alleged killer could not imagine how the city of Charleston, under the good and wise leadership of Mayor Riley—(*applause*)—how the state of South Carolina, how the United States of America would respond—not merely with revulsion at his evil act, but with big-hearted generosity and, more importantly, with a thoughtful introspection and self-examination that we so rarely see in public life.

Blinded by hatred, he failed to comprehend what Reverend Pinckney so well understood—the power of God's grace. (*Applause.*)

This whole week, I've been reflecting on this idea of grace. (*Applause.*) The grace of the families who lost loved ones. The grace that Reverend Pinckney would preach about in his sermons. The grace described in one of my favorite hymnals [sic]—the one we all know.

> Amazing grace! (how sweet the sound)
> That sav'd a wretch, like me! (*Applause.*)

I once was lost, but now am found,
Was blind, but now I see. (*Applause.*)[5]

According to the Christian tradition, grace is not earned. Grace is not merited. It's not something we deserve. Rather, grace is the free and benevolent favor of God—(*applause*)—as manifested in the salvation of sinners and the bestowal of blessings.[6] Grace.

As a nation, out of this terrible tragedy, God has visited grace upon us, for he has allowed us to see where we've been blind. (*Applause.*) He has given us the chance, where we've been lost, to find our best selves. (*Applause.*) We may not have earned it, this grace, with our rancor and complacency and short-sightedness and fear of each other, but we got it all the same. He gave it to us anyway. He's once more given us grace. But it is up to us now to make the most of it, to receive it with gratitude, and to prove ourselves worthy of this gift.

For too long, we were blind to the pain that the Confederate flag stirred in too many of our citizens. (*Applause.*) It's true, a flag did not cause these murders. But as people from all walks of life, Republicans and

---

[5]John Newton, Faith's review and expectation, v. 1, John Newton/ William Cowper, *Olney Hymns in Three Books* (London: W. Oliver, 1779), book 1, hymn 41 (pp. 53-54). By the time he wrote this hymn, Newton had given up the transatlantic slave trade for the Anglican priesthood. Many years later, he became an outspoken abolitionist.

[6]C.f., Romans 5:1-5. Obama may have intended to provide not only an assurance of grace (5:1-2) but also a salvific perspective on the audience's trauma (5:3-5).

Democrats, now acknowledge—including Governor Haley, whose recent eloquence on the subject is worthy of praise—(*applause*)—as we all have to acknowledge, the flag has always represented more than just ancestral pride. (*Applause.*) For many, black and white, that flag was a reminder of systemic oppression and racial subjugation. We see that now.

Removing the flag from this state's capitol would not be an act of political correctness; it would not be an insult to the valor of Confederate soldiers. It would simply be an acknowledgement that the cause for which they fought—the cause of slavery—was wrong—(*applause*)—the imposition of Jim Crow after the Civil War, the resistance to civil rights for all people was wrong. (*Applause.*) It would be one step in an honest accounting of America's history; a modest but meaningful balm for so many unhealed wounds.[7] It would be an expression of the amazing changes that have transformed this state and this country for the better, because of the work of so many people of goodwill, people of all races striving to form a more perfect union. By taking down that flag, we express God's grace. (*Applause.*)

But I don't think God wants us to stop there. (*Applause.*) For too long, we've been blind to the way past injustices continue to shape the present. Perhaps we see that now. Perhaps this tragedy causes us to ask some tough questions about how we can permit so many of our children

---

[7] C.f., Hymn text: There is a balm in Gilead (anonymous 19th century African American spiritual).

to languish in poverty, or attend dilapidated schools, or grow up without prospects for a job or for a career. (*Applause.*)

Perhaps it causes us to examine what we're doing to cause some of our children to hate. (*Applause.*) Perhaps it softens hearts towards those lost young men, tens and tens of thousands caught up in the criminal justice system— (*applause*)—and leads us to make sure that the system is not infected with bias; that we embrace changes in how we train and equip our police so that the bonds of trust between law enforcement and the communities they serve make us all safer and more secure. (*Applause.*)

Maybe we now realize the way racial bias can infect us, even when we don't realize it, so that we're guarding against not just racial slurs, but we're also guarding against the subtle impulse to call Johnny back for a job interview but not Jamal. (*Applause.*) So that we search our hearts when we consider laws to make it harder for some of our fellow citizens to vote. (*Applause.*) By recognizing our common humanity, by treating every child as important, regardless of the color of their skin or the station into which they were born, and to do what's necessary to make opportunity real for every American—by doing that, we express God's grace. (*Applause.*)

For too long...

AUDIENCE: For too long!

OBAMA

For too long, we've been blind to the unique mayhem that gun violence inflicts upon this nation. (*Applause.*) Sporadically, our eyes are open: When eight of our brothers and sisters are cut down in a church basement, twelve in a movie theater, 26 in an elementary school. But I hope we also see the thirty precious lives cut short by gun violence in this country every single day; the countless more those lives are forever changed—the survivors crippled, the children traumatized and fearful every day as they walk to school, the husband who will never feel his wife's warm touch, the entire communities whose grief overflows every time they have to watch what happened to them happen to some other place.

The vast majority of Americans—the majority of gun owners—want to do something about this. We see that now. (*Applause.*) And I'm convinced that by acknowledging the pain and loss of others, even as we respect the traditions and ways of life that make up this beloved country—by making the moral choice to change, we express God's grace. (*Applause.*)

We don't earn grace. We're all sinners. We don't deserve it. (*Applause.*) But God gives it to us anyway. (*Applause.*) And we choose how to receive it. It's our decision how to honor it.

None of us can or should expect a transformation in race relations overnight. Every time something like this happens, somebody says we have to have a conversation about race. We talk a lot about race. There's no shortcut.

And we don't need more talk. (*Applause.*) None of us should believe that a handful of gun safety measures will prevent every tragedy. It will not. People of goodwill will continue to debate the merits of various policies, as our democracy requires—this is a big, raucous place, America is. And there are good people on both sides of these debates. Whatever solutions we find will necessarily be incomplete.

But it would be a betrayal of everything Reverend Pinckney stood for, I believe, if we allowed ourselves to slip into a comfortable silence again. (*Applause.*) Once the eulogies have been delivered, once the TV cameras move on, to go back to business as usual—that's what we so often do to avoid uncomfortable truths about prejudice that still infect our society. (*Applause.*) To settle for symbolic gestures without following up with the hard work of more lasting change—that's how we lose our way again.

It would be a refutation of the forgiveness expressed by those families if we merely slipped into old habits, whereby those who disagree with us are not merely wrong but bad; where we shout instead of listen; where we barricade ourselves behind preconceived notions or well-practiced cynicism.

Reverend Pinckney once said, "Across the South, we have a deep appreciation of history—we haven't always had a deep appreciation of each other's history." (*Applause.*) What is true in the South is true for America. Clem understood that justice grows out of recognition of ourselves in each other. That my liberty depends on you being free, too. (*Applause.*) That history can't be a sword to justify injustice, or a shield against progress, but must be a manual for how to avoid repeating the mistakes of the past—how to break the cycle. A roadway toward a better world. He knew that the path of grace involves an open mind—but, more importantly, an open heart.

That's what I've felt this week—an open heart. That, more than any particular policy or analysis, is what's called upon right now, I think—what a friend of mine, the writer Marilynne Robinson, calls "the reservoir of goodness, beyond, and of another kind, that we are able to do each other in the ordinary cause of things.[8]"

That reservoir of goodness. If we can find that grace, anything is possible. (*Applause.*) If we can tap that grace, everything can change. (*Applause.*)

Amazing grace. Amazing grace.

[*Begins to sing.*]
Amazing grace! (*Applause.*) (how sweet the sound)
That sav'd a wretch, like me!
I once was lost, but now am found,
Was blind, but now I see. (*Applause.*)[9]

Clementa Pinckney found that grace.
Cynthia Hurd found that grace.

---

[8]As in https://www.goodreads.com/quotes/7139789-that-reservoir-of-goodness-beyond-and-of-another-kind-that (accessed August 11, 2019).

[9]Newton, Faith's review and expectation, v. 1, *Olney hymns*, 1:53.

Susie Jackson found that grace.
Ethel Lance found that grace.
DePayne Middleton-Doctor found that grace.
Tywanza Sanders found that grace.
Daniel L. Simmons, Sr. found that grace.
Sharonda Coleman-Singleton found that grace.
Myra Thompson found that grace.

Through the example of their lives, they've now passed it on to us. May we find ourselves worthy of that precious and extraordinary gift, as long as our lives endure.[10] May grace now lead them home.[11] May God continue to shed his grace on the United States of America. (*Applause.*)

---

[10]C.f., "…as long as life endures." Newton, Faith's review and expectation (Amazing Grace), v. 4, *Olney hymns*, 1:54.

[11]C.f., "…and grace will lead me home." Newton, Faith's review and expectation (Amazing Grace), v. 3, *Olney hymns*, 1:54.

Emanuel African Methodist Episcopal Church, Charleston, SC (courtesy Richard Ellis/Alamy Stock Photo).

9

The Dying Thief:
Eulogy for Wash Moore

POMPEY
SPRINGVALE AFRICAN METHODIST EPISCOPAL CHURCH
FAIRFIELD COUNTY, SC

During the 1930's, Franklin Roosevelt attempted to alleviate the extreme unemployment that plagued virtually all segments of society during the Great Depression. His administration created two programs to provide public-sector jobs, which, in turn, might provide money that wage earners might spend at privately owned businesses. Both the Civilian Conservation Corps and the Works Progress Administration used Keynesian, demand-side economic stimulus in an attempt to rejuvenate the economy.
Within the Works Progress Administration, the Federal Writers' Project hired unemployed writers to interview elderly persons and commit their memories to

writing. Among the interviewees, former slaves rapidly became a population of particular interest. While many former slaves remained alive more than 70 years after the thirteenth amendment was ratified, one could not fail to observe that this population was ageing and that its numbers were declining rapidly.

William Woodward Dixon, an elderly, Caucasian resident of Fairfield County, SC participated in the Federal Writers' Project. He either sought out or was matched with Ned Walker, an even older ex-slave from the same county. During their conversations, it became apparent that Walker had been acquainted with Dixon's grandfather, William B. Woodward. Moreover, the two families' narratives intersected most strongly at a funeral preached by Pompey, an individual whom Walker identified as an "uncle."

By the time they conducted their interviews (1936-1938), both participants had long histories in Fairfield County. The 1870 census indicates that Dixon, then about two years of age, was raised by his grandfather, Walker's acquaintance.[1] Woodward was listed as a farmer with a personal estate valued at $1,200 but was denied the franchise for some reason other than crime or rebellion. Dixon's parents, Sallie and Samuel, do not appear in the 1870 census.

---

[1] 1870 US census, William B. Woodward family entries, Fairfield County, SC, township 2, p. 18, lines 9-17.

POMPEY: THE DYING THIEF

Walker's story appears in the narrative. This story expresses a surprisingly positive opinion of his owners, the Gaillards. On the one hand, the extent to which Walker and/or Dixon attempted to perpetuate the stereotype of the happy slave is unknown. On the other hand, Walker's narrative and the probable circumstances of the sale of the Gaillards' Spring Vale plantation to the former slaves provide partial explanations for this positive relationship.

Walker's father was the family's coachman at both upstate locations, the Spring Vale plantation and the Clifton Place town home. In addition, he served as valet, taking care of the Gaillard children. Walker's mother also had a supervisory role. She managed the slave workforce in the weave house. Walker's experience as a member of a family in the higher rungs of the Gaillard estate's servile hierarchy colored his opinion of his former owners.

Since South Carolina had seceded from the union, the Emancipation Proclamation theoretically had freed the slaves in 1863. The narrative implies that the vast majority of the slaves remained at Spring Vale. By the end of the war, the Gaillard daughters had married and the surviving sons were beginning to live their own lives after military service to the Confederacy. David Gaillard had died in 1855, and the widowed Louisa, beginning the last decades of her life, had a secure upstate residence at Clifton Place. In short, the circumstances suggest that Spring Vale had become surplus property, no longer much of an asset, for the Gaillards.

The thirteenth amendment facilitated the sale of Spring Vale (the 1,385 acres on Wateree Creek) to the former slaves on the installment plan. This constitutional amendment both ratified the former slaves' free status and provided legal warrant for them to enter contracts and incur financial obligations.

Henry Gaillard presumably realized that he could use the former slaves' new legal status to his family's advantage. By registering the slaves and giving each head of household his own name, Gaillard provided the legal foundation required for the slaves to become parties to an enforceable contract. The sale of Spring Vale apparently benefitted both parties in roughly equal measure. This observation indicates that the transaction was at arm's length, with neither party under inordinate pressure to consummate the arrangement. Furthermore, the sale falls within Henry and Louisa Gaillard's practice of real estate divestiture after David Gaillard's death, as documented by several Fairfield County deeds.

Nevertheless, Henry Gaillard maintained one key advantage. The Fairfield County deeds do not include any documentation of the transaction that Walker described. This absence indicates that the sale transpired in much the same manner as do owner-financed transactions today. The Gaillards retained title while the former slaves were making their payments. Walker indicated that the sale met a need for both parties during the short term, and the Gaillards' normal real estate practices after 1855 corroborate this impression. Since the interview focused on

Walker's experience during Reconstruction (1865-1876), it includes no indication of the sale's longer-term results.

The Walker narrative, in its current form,[2] is a literary creation, presumably finalized by Dixon with Walker's cooperation. The Library of Congress typescript demarcates the paragraphs not only with the customary indentation but also with quotation marks. This feature, unusual outside of the Federal Writers' Project narratives, suggests that the account was assembled from non-adjacent interview excerpts, arranged topically. The narrative culminates with the intersection of the two interview participants' family histories at Wash Moore's funeral. It concludes immediately with differing opinions of the preacher's technique by the interviewer's grandfather and the grandfather's nephew.

The literary structure of the Library of Congress typescript resembles a more primitive version of William Faulkner's stream of consciousness technique. The story has two plots. The later plot, embedded in the setting, focuses on the speculation by Dixon and Walker about the beginning of the pension payments promised by the Social Security Act. The second, described by Walker, relates to the family's transition in place from slavery to freedom. The two plots intersect with the interviewer's grandfather's

---

[2]"Ned Walker" (project 1655), Federal Writers' Project, *Slave narrative project*, v. 14, South Carolina, Part 4, Raines-Young, pp. 174-180. Washington DC: United States Works Projects Administration Records, Manuscript Division, Library of Congress, 1941.

response to a funeral sermon by an individual whom the interviewee identified with the title "uncle."

Walker apparently was a chain smoker. He used the promise of more information to obtain more cigarettes from Dixon, holding out for one final cigarette before telling Dixon about the funeral in which two of Dixon's relatives had participated.

"Uncle" Pompey was associated with a Springvale African Methodist Episcopal Church. Current Fairfield County residents and descendants of the families in the narrative are not aware of any traditions pertaining to the church. The most that can be said is that it was named after and presumably located on the former site of the Spring Vale plantation. Whether the church became defunct, was absorbed into a current congregation, or met some other fate is not known at this point. Some AME and AME Zion congregations are located in Fairfield County. Walker's remains and those of his wife and two daughters are buried in Bethel AME Zion's cemetery.

While the fate of the Springvale congregation is not known, the religious training of some of its members is clear. During the interviews, Walker praised his former owners and, by implication, their church, St. John's Episcopal, Winnsboro, SC, for steering a middle course between the extremes of Calvinistic (hard shell) and Arminian (soft shell) practice. He noted that the former slaves who constituted the Springvale church desired to maintain some of the doctrine and polity of the former owners' church while striking out on their own regarding hymnody and presumably other aspects of worship style.

Walker identified Pompey with the title "uncle." As a slave, he had been called Dan. When Henry Gaillard helped the ex-slaves register as residents in their own right, he gave Dan the name Pompey. The 1870 census records three African American residents with this name who were old enough to be heads of household around 1865, when Henry Gaillard summoned them to town to receive their new names and register. Pompey Henry and Pompey Veal were illiterate farm laborers with no estate the census takers considered worth quantifying. Pompey Aiken, in contrast, was literate, and had an estate of $125.[3] He was not upper class; his wife and child are listed as illiterate farm laborers. However, he seems more prepared than the other two Pompeys to have delivered a sermon derived from a scripture text, used a sophisticated type of logic, matched both the decedent's circumstances and the logic of the scripture passage to an Anglican hymn text, and included a play on words.

The most likely origin of Pompey Aiken's surname is that of James Aiken, another Fairfield County landowner and St. John Episcopal parishioner. James Aiken named his daughter after Louisa Gaillard. The remains of Louisa Gaillard Aiken, who was born and died in 1855, are buried in the St. John churchyard, the same cemetery in which

---

[3] 1870 US Census, Pompey Aiken family entries, Fairfield County, SC, township 8, p. 11, line 40 – p. 12, lines 1-2.

David Gaillard's remains were buried, also in 1855. While the strongest likelihood is that Pompey assumed his former owner's surname, Henry Gaillard's random assignment of names to his family's former slaves precludes ruling out the possibility that he reciprocated the recognition James Aiken provided for Henry's mother. We can conclude only that Pompey shared a personal (first) name and probably also a socioeconomic status with Pompey Aiken. In any case, his eulogy reflects a complex arrangement of components on the basis of an abstract logical strategy.

Walker gave not only Pompey but also the deceased Wash Moore the title "uncle." Walker's narrative neither necessitates nor precludes any of the following three uses of the term: (1) A description of a biological relationship, (2) An honorific title given to an older, African American male, and (3) An indication that Walker construed the former Gaillard slaves at Spring Vale and their associates as a fictive kinship group. The social organization within communities of former slaves, such as Walker's associates, lies beyond the scope of the current volume but could be a fruitful avenue of inquiry.

The description of the funeral focuses on the final burst of visual and musical imagery and says very little about the earlier portions of the sermon. Walker noted that Pompey derived the sermon from a text about Paul and Silas being imprisoned (Acts 16:23-26 and possibly some subsequent verses). While the bulk of the sermon is undescribed, the use of the text implies an argumentum a fortiori *(from greater to lesser). The example of Paul and*

Silas, acknowledged early Christian leaders, being imprisoned opened the possibility of lesser Christians being redeemed after imprisonment.

The second verse of "There is a fountain filled with blood" parallels the Acts passage logically and thus reinforces the deductive rhetoric by adding an inductive argument. This text compares the crucified and redeemed bandit of Luke 23:43 (dying thief in the hymn text) to the Christian who might wash all his sins away in the cleansing fountain. The logical progression culminates with the visual image of Wash Moore climbing Jacob's ladder successfully as the funeralgoers sang.

Pompey's sermon recalled homiletical techniques of an earlier era and anticipated approaches popularized during Walker's final years by the pastoral care movement. The sermon addressed Wash Moore's status as a convicted larcenist explicitly but emphasized the good he did in his job as a blacksmith. In this respect, it was ahead of its time. The manner of soliciting audience participation at the end resembled camp meeting techniques from the Second Great Awakening, depicted verbally in the hymn text, "Brethren, we have met together."

Walker noted that both African Americans and Caucasians participated in the funeral. Moore presumably served any customer who could afford to pay his price, with some of these customers being Caucasian. Whether or not Pompey's multi-faceted preaching may have gained him a following among residents of both races is unknown.

The Federal Writers' Project typescript, reproduced below, is a product of the 1930's. One of its notable characteristics is the frequent representation of the soft "th" diphthong as "d." The consistent use of this transliteration leads me to suspect that Walker may have been unable to pronounce the diphthong, owing to the loss of one or more upper, front teeth. In addition, the typescript includes Walker's references to himself and his relatives in terms that contemporary readers may find offensive. I have given the sermon a title, derived from the decisive hymn verse, and have provided the scripture text which Pompey used, according to Walker's recollection.

> After they whipped Paul and Silas severely, they threw them into prison and reminded the warden to guard them carefully. When he received this warning, he incarcerated them in the maximum security cellblock and fastened their feet in the stocks. About midnight, as Paul and Silas were praying and singing hymns to God, the other inmates were listening to them. Then a sudden earthquake shook the foundations of the prison so severely that all of the doors were opened immediately and all of the prisoners' chains were released.
>
> Acts 16:23-26

INTERVIEWER'S FORWARD

Ned Walker lives in the village of White Oak, near Winnsboro, SC, in a two-room frame house, the dwelling of his son-in-law, Leander Heath, who married his daughter Nora. Ned is too old to do any work of a remunerative character but looks after the garden and chickens of his daughter and son-in-law. He is a frequent visitor to Winnsboro, SC. He brings chickens and garden produce, to sell in the town and the Winnsboro Mill's village. He is tall, thin, and straight, with kind eyes. Being one of the old Gaillard Negroes, transplanted from the Santee section of Berkeley County, in the Low Country, to the red hills of Fairfield County, in the Up Country, he still retains words and phrases characteristic of the Negro in the lower part of South Carolina.[4]

WILLIAM WOODWARD DIXON

Yes sir, I's tall and slim lak a saplin'; maybe dat a good reason I live so long. Doctor say lean people lives longer than fat people.

I hear daddy read one time from de Bible 'bout a man havin' strength of years in his right hand and honor and riches in his left hand, but whenever I open dat left hand dere is nothin' in it. 'Spect dat promise is comin' tho', when the old age pension money gits down here from Washington. When you 'spect it is comin'? De palm of my hand sho' begin to itch for dat greenback money. So you think it's on de way? Well, thank God for dat but it

---

[4]Ned Walker's assertion (142) that he was born on Clifton Place, in the southeast corner of Winnsboro, SC, contradicts William Dixon's claim (above) that Walker was born in South Carolina's coastal region and transplanted to Winnsboro. Walker's 1957 death certificate identifies his birthplace simply as South Carolina.

seem 'most too good to be true.⁵ Now I'll quit askin' questions and just set here and smoke and answer whilst you do de puttin' down on de paper.

Yes sir, I was born right here in de southeast corner of Winnsboro, on de Clifton Place. De day I was born, it b'long to my master, David Gaillard. Miss Louisa, dat's Master David's wife, 'low to me one day, "Ned, don't you ever call de master, old master, and don't you ever think of me as old miss'." I promise her dat I keep dat always in mind, and I ain't gonna change, though she done gone to heaven and is in de choir a singin' and a singin' them chants dat her could pipe so pretty at St. John's, in Winnsboro. You see they was 'Piscopalians. Dere was no hard shell Baptist and no soft shell Methodist in deir make up. It was all glory, big glory, glory in de very highest rung of Jacob's ladder,⁶ wid our white folks.

Well, how I is ramblin'. You see dere was Master David and Mistress Louisa, de king bee and de queen bee. They had a plantation down on de Santee, in the Low Country, somewhere 'bout Moncks Corner. One day Master David buy a 1,385 acres on Wateree Creek. He also

---

⁵The Federal Writers' Project interviews occurred between 1936 and 1938. Walker's comments indicate that he was aware that the Social Security Act had become law in 1935 but uncertain about the timing of the payments prescribed by the new law. The first social security checks were issued in 1940, two years after the interviews concluded.

⁶Genesis 28:10-19 was a vision illustrating postexilic Jewish territorial aspirations. Since there was no independent Jewish state between 63 BCE and 1947, Walker and Pompey, reinterpreted the vision in terms of their Christian beliefs in heavenly glory and the afterlife.

buy de Clifton Place, to live in, in Winnsboro. I can't git my mind back to tell you what I wants for you to put on de paper. 'Scuse me, forgit everything, 'till you git my pedigree down.

I done name Master David and Mistress Louisa. Now for de chillun. Us was told to front de boys name wid Marse and de young ladies name wid Miss. Now us can go and git somewhere.

Well, dere was Miss Elizabeth; she marry Mr. Dwight. Miss Maria marry another Mr. Dwight. Miss Kate marry Mr. Bob Ellison, a sheriff. Her got two chillum in Columbia, Marse David and Marse DuBose Ellison. Then for de boys; they all went to de war. Marse Alley got kilt. Marse Dick rise to be a captain and after de war marry Congressman Boyce's daughter, Miss Fannie. Marse Ike marry and live in de Low Country; he die 'bout two years ago. Marse Sam marry a Miss DuBose and went wid General Wade Hampton.

Marse Sam's son cut out a canal that divide half and half de western part of de whole world. Us niggers was powerful scared, 'til Marse David Gaillard took a hold of de business. Why us scared? Why us fear dat de center of de backbone of de world down dere, when cut, would tipple over lak de halfs of a watermelon and everybody would go under de water in de ocean. How could Marse David prevent it? Us niggers of de Gaillard generation have confidence in de Gaillard race and us willin' to sink or swim wid them in whatever they do. Young Marse David propped de sides of de world up all right, down dere, and they name a big part of dat canal, Gaillard Cut, so they did. (Gaillard Cut,[7] Panama Canal)

Well, I keep a ramblin'. Will I ever git to Marse Henry, de one dat looked after and cared for slaves of de family most and best? Marse Henry marry a Miss White in Charleston. He rise to be a captain and adjutant of de fighting 6th Regiment. After de war him fix it so de slaves stay altogether, on dat 1,385 acres and buy de place, as common tenants, on de 'stallment plan. He send word for de head of each family to come to Winnsboro; us to have names and register. Marse Henry command; us obey. Dat was a great day. My daddy already had his name, Tom. He was de driver of de buggy, de carriage, and one of de wagons, in slavery. Marse Henry wrote him a name on a slip and say: "Tom, as you have never walked much, I name you Walker."

It wasn't long befo' daddy, who was de only one dat could read and write, ride down to Columbia and come back wid a 'mission in his pocket from de 'Publican governor, to be Justice of de Peace.

Marse Henry ladle out some "golliwhopshus" names dat day. Such as: Caesar Harrison, Edward Cades, and Louis Brevard. He say, "Louis, I give you de name of a judge. Dan, I give you a Roman name, Pompey." Pompey turned out to be a preacher and I see your grandpa,

---

[7]Now known as Culebra Cut or Corte de Culebra. David Dubose Gaillard (1859-1913), the Army Corps of Engineers officer largely responsible for the excavation of that part of the Panama Canal, was a grandson of Ned Walker's former owners. The information in parentheses is presumed to be Dixon's editorial comment.

Marse William Woodward, in de graveyard when Uncle Pompey preached de funeral of old Uncle Wash Moore. Tell you 'bout dat if I has time.

Well, he give Uncle Sam de name of Shadrock. When he reach Uncle Aleck, he 'low: "I adds to your name Aleck, two fine names, a preacher's and a scholar's, Porter Ramsey." 'Bout dat time a little runt elbow and butt his way right up to de front and say, "Marse Henry, Marse Henry! I wants a big bulldozin' name." Marse Henry look at him and say, "You little shrimp, take dis then." And Marse Henry write on de slip of paper: Mendoza J. Fernandez, and read it out loud. De little runt laugh mighty pleased and some of them Fernandezes 'round here to dis day.

My mammy name Bess, my granddaddy name June, grandmammy Renah, but all my brothers dead. My sisters Clerissie and Phibbie am still livin'. Us was born in a two-story frame house, chimney in de middle, four rooms downstairs and four upstairs. Dere was four families livin' in it. Dese was de town domestics of master. Him have another residence on de plantation and a set of domestics, but my daddy was de coachman for both places.

De Gaillard quarters was a little town laid out wid streets wide 'nough for a wagon to pass thru. Houses was on each side of de street. A well and church was in de center of de town. Dere was a gin-house, barns, stables, cowpen, and a big bell on top of a high pole at de barn gate. Dere was a big trough at de well, kept full of water day and night, in case of fire and to water de stock. Us had peg beds, wheat straw mattress, and rag pillows. Cotton was too valuable.

Master didn't 'low de chillum to be worked. He feed slaves on 'tatoes, rice, corn pone, hominy, fried meat, 'lasses, shorts, turnips, collards, and string beans. Us had pumpkin pie on Sunday. No butter, no sweet milk, but us got blabber and buttermilk.

Oh, then, I 'bout to forgit. Dere was a big hall wid spinnin' wheels in it, where thread was spin. Dat thread was hauled to Winnsboro and brought to de Clifton place in Winnsboro, to de weave house. Dat house set 'bout where de Winnsboro Mill is now. Mammy was head of de weave house force and see to de cloth. Dere was a dye-room down dere too. They use red earth sometime and sometime walnut stain. My mammy learn all dis from a white lady, Miss Spurrier, dat Master David put in charge dere at first. How long she stay? I disremembers dat. Us no want for clothes summer or winter. Had wooden bottom shoes, two pair in a year.

Mr. Sam Johnson was de overseer. Dere was 'bout 700 slaves in de Gaillard quarter and twenty in town, countin' de chillun. De young white marsters break de law when they teach daddy to read and write. Marse Dick say: "To hell wid de law, I got to have somebody dat can read and write 'mong de servants." My daddy was his valet. He put de boys to bed, put on deir shoes and brush them off, and all dat kind of 'tention.

De church was called Springvale. After freedom, by a vote, de members jines up, out of respect to de family, wid de African Methodist 'Piscopalian Church, so as to have as much of de form, widout de substance of them chants, of de master's church.

No sir, us had no mulattoes on de place. Everybody decent and happy. They give us two days durin' Christmas for celebratin' and dancin'.

I marry Sylvin Field, a gal on de General Bratton Canaan place.[8] Us have three chillum. Nora Heath, dat I'm now livin' wid, at White Oak, Bessie Lew, in Tennessee, and Susannah, who is dead.[9]

What I think of Abe Lincoln? Dat was a mighty man of de Lord. What I think of Jeff Davis? He all right, 'cordin' to his education, just lak my white folks. What I think of Mr. Roosevelt? O man! Dat's our papa.

Go off! I's blabbed 'nough. You 'bliged to hear 'bout dat funeral? Will I pester you for 'nother cigarette? No sir! I ain't gonna smoke it lak you smoke it. Supposin' us was settin' here smokin' them de same? A Gaillard come up them steps and see us. He say: "Shame on dat white man," turn his back, and walk back down. A Woodward come up them steps and see us. He say: "You d— nigger! What's all dis?" Take me by de collar, boot me down them steps, and come back and have it out wid you. Dat's 'bout de difference of de up and low country buckra.

---

[8] Sylvia (1870-1940), according to her headstone in Bethel AME Zion Cemetery on US 321 south of Woodward, SC.

[9] Variant spelling, Susana, is on headstone in Bethel AME Zion Cemetery.

Now 'bout Uncle Wash's funeral. Uncle Wash was de blacksmith in de forks of de road 'cross de railroad from Concord Church.[10] He was a powerful man! Him use de hammer and tongs for all de people miles and miles 'round. Him jine de Springvale African Methodist 'Piscopalian Church, but fell from grace. Him covet a hog of Marse Walt Brice[11] and was sent to de penitentiary for two years, 'bout dat hog. Him contacted [sic] consumption down dere and come home.[12] His chest was all sunk in and his ribs full of rheumatism. Him soon went to bed and died. Him was buried on top of de hill, in de pines just north of Woodward. Uncle Pompey preached de funeral. White folks was dere. Marse William was dere, and his nephew, de Attorney General of Arizona.[13] Uncle Pompey took his

---

[10]Probably the Concord Presbyterian Church building, an 1818 structure still standing beside highway 321 and the railroad tracks in Fairfield County, SC, between Winnsboro and Woodward.

[11]A physician and farmer who lived in the same township as William Woodward. The 1870 census (Fairfield County, SC, township 2, p. 43, line 35) valued his real estate holdings at $8,400 and his personal property at $1,075.

[12]"Contacted" is a typographical error for "contracted". Consumption is known today as tuberculosis. Since it is contagious and was untreatable before the development of antibiotics, Wash Moore may have been released early to avert the risk he might have posed to the other inmates as he served out what, for all practical purposes, was the capital sentence imposed by the disease.

[13]Ned Walker previously identified William Woodward as the grandfather of his interviewer, William Dixon. As Woodward's nephew, Tom (the Arizona attorney general) also was a Dixon relative.

text 'bout Paul and Silas layin' in jail and dat it was not 'ternally against a church member to go to jail. Him dwell on de life of labor and bravery, in tacklin' kickin' hosses and mules. How him sharpen de dull plow points and make de corn and cotton grow, to feed and clothe de hungry and naked. He look up thru de pine tree tops and say, "I see Jacob's ladder. Brother Wash is climbin' dat ladder. Him is halfway up. Ah! Brudders and sisters, pray, while I preach, dat he enter in them pearly gates. I see them gates open. Brother Wash done reach de topmost rung in dat ladder. Let us sing, wid a shout, dat blessed hymn, 'Dere Is a Fountain Filled Wid Blood.'"[14] Wid de first verse de women got to hollerin' and wid de second, Uncle Pompey say: "De dyin' thief, I see him dere to welcome Brother Wash in paradise. Thank God! Brother Wash done washed as white as snow and landed safe forevermore."

Dat Attorney General turn up his coat in de November wind and say: "I'll be damn!" Marse William smile and 'low: "O Tom! Don't be too hard on them. 'Member he will have mercy on them, dat have mercy on others."

---

[14]Text by William Cowper: "There is a fountain filled with blood," in Richard Conyers, *A collection of psalms and hymns from various authors: For the use of serious and devout Christians of all denominations* (London: Clement Watts, 1772). By 1850, when Lowell Mason and George Webb republished Mason's setting of the hymn in *Cantica Laudis*, v. 2 had achieved its current form: "The dying thief rejoiced to see / That fountain in his day. / And there may I, though vile as he, / Wash all my sins away."

Headstones mark the graves of Ned Walker, his wife, two of their three daughters, and their grandson in Bethel AME Zion Cemetery, Fairfield County, SC (Photos courtesy Green Giebner).

10

Smoketown Get-Down Welcome Remarks

RANDALL C. WEBBER
SMOKETOWN NEIGHBORHOOD ASSOCIATION, INC.
LOUISVILLE, KY

Smoketown, Louisville's oldest African American neighborhood, holds a block party each September. This festive occasion usually begins with a brief, upbeat welcome. Unfortunately, the circumstances preceding the 2016 event necessitated a more somber demeanor. About two months earlier, a pair of shootings on consecutive days killed three young residents. Residents speculated openly that the second shooting, which killed both combatants, was retributory. The local police did not comment on this issue. On the one hand, they needed to protect the integrity of their investigation; on the other hand, their reticence exacerbated the residents' concerns.

Smoketown's tragedies were not limited to the two shootings. A month and a half earlier, the best known of the boxers to have learned the sport in Smoketown died, following a period of declining health. About a year before the party, a then-resident published a book about her escort service, emphasizing her business relationship with a local university's basketball program. In light of this rapid succession of tragedies, the residents had ample reason to wonder about both the competence and the diligence with which I managed their concerns.

Before the block party, I had said very little publicly about the tragedies. I had given Metro Council's public safety committee chair my recommendations regarding the escort service but had refrained from additional public comment. After the shootings, I did some press interviews in which I urged the local police to find an appropriate line between the residents' needs for reassurance regarding their safety and the risk of being perceived as overly aggressive. In many of Louisville's African American neighborhoods, including Smoketown, mutual trust between residents and police is built with difficulty and shaken easily.

The welcome address provided an opportunity for public comment after the need for crisis management was past. With about two months to reflect on the tragedies, I could use techniques from funerals I have officiated to reflect on the neighborhood's difficulties and encourage the residents to engage in uplifting behaviors.

The first issue I needed to address was the difficulty of enabling myself and the audience to identify with each other. The block party's attendance is drawn heavily from the neighborhood's younger residents, most of whom are not well-to-do financially. In contrast, I am a middle-aged, middle class Caucasian. I managed the risk posed by the age, economic, and racial differences between me and most listeners by acknowledging those differences implicitly. I accomplished this goal by devising the welcome as a short, deliberative speech to those who could be considered my peers, at least in terms of age and experience. During the speech, I referred to the actual listeners in the third person to create the impression that I was speaking to their elders and allowing the listeners to eavesdrop.

The welcome was neither a funeral nor a memorial service. However, it memorialized a number of individuals, some living and others deceased, who were associated with Smoketown. It referred to the neighborhood's difficulties elliptically, only after noting the accomplishments of those whom it memorialized. This strategy established a foundation for the subsequent challenge to the audience to display responsible behaviors that might strengthen the community.

The speech was clearly secular. One of the positive examples was a boxer who became an Islamic pacifist. The model for the conclusion was a cemetery dedication speech by a Republican politician from rural LaRue County. Even as a secular composition, though, the speech relied heavily on imagery from the Judeo-Christian scriptural heritage and Protestant hymnody, as indicated in the notes.

The audience seemed to appreciate the speech. More importantly, Smoketown avoided fatal shootings for almost three years after the speech, and the community seems to be evolving in a positive direction. One cannot attribute any success to my monotone delivery, the familiar content, or the lack of specific policy proposals. Success is a byproduct of a speech that reflected the mood of many in the community after several sad events occurred in rapid succession.

On behalf of Kentuckians for the Commonwealth and Smoketown Neighborhood Association, I am pleased to welcome you to the third annual Get-Down. Earlier today we rededicated the Unity Monument at Lampton and Hancock Streets. This impressionistic sculpture is in the shape of a pair of boxing gloves brought together to form a heart. At this time we wish to express our gratitude for those who have gone before us[1] and have served as our examples, beginning with the boxers. We are grateful for Fred Stoner, who taught generations of boys both boxing and citizenship. We are equally grateful for the contributions that his former students have made beyond their sport. Consider the following former boxers, some well-known, others obscure:

---

[1] "B.C." (attrib. Benjamin Clark), Hymn text: On seeing a mourning ring inscribed with the words, "Not lost, but gone before," *Evangelical Magazine*, 1820.

Marshall Gazaway, who is striving to bring new life to the property previously intended for use as the west Louisville foodport;

Jimmy Ellis, who helped his church members teach homeless children to read music even while he was fighting cognitive impairments;

Muhammad Ali, whose Islamic pacifism provided an alternative both to American militarism and to the brutality of some Muslims.

We are grateful not only for our boxers but for all current and former Smoketown residents who have contributed to our community: For Elmer Lucille Allen, one of Louisville's first African American female chemists, for Smoketown Pride & Heritage founder Ruby Hyde; and for Zephra Mae Miller, the artist who designed the Unity Monument.[2]

As the number of our predecessors dwindles and the younger generations become more prominent, our neighborhood is approaching a turning point. We may walk the broad road of self-aggrandizement and retribution, which leads to death. Alternatively, wisdom shows us a narrow path of self-sacrifice and forbearance, which leads to renewed life.[3]

---

[2] Roster modeled on Hebrews 11:1-40.

[3] Isaac Watts, Hymn text: The almost Christian (Broad is the road that leads to death). *Hymns and Spiritual Songs*, 1707-1709, c.f., Matthew 7:13-14.

Earlier today, we rededicated the Unity Monument. In a larger sense, however, we cannot rededicate this monument. Those whose accomplishments the monument commemorates have dedicated it already, far beyond our ability to add or detract. Rather, let us dedicate ourselves to the healing of Smoketown's and Louisville's injuries.[4] Since we are surrounded by a large crowd of spectators, let us shed every encumbrance and persevere in running the race before us[5] so future generations might beat their swords into ploughshares, their spears into pruning hooks,[6] and sing, "There is a balm in Gilead, to make the wounded whole."[7]

---

[4]Modeled on Abraham Lincoln, *Address delivered at the dedication of the cemetery at Gettysburg*, signed 11/19/1863 manuscript, cols. 1-2 (https://gettysburg150concerts.files.wordpress.com/2012/11/gettysburg-address2.jpg, accessed 11/26/2017).

[5]Hebrews 12:1.

[6]Isaiah 2:4.

[7]Anonymous hymn text: There is a balm in Gilead, 19th century African-American spiritual.

Works Cited

A Call to Conscience: The Landmark Speeches of Dr. Martin Luther King, Jr. (2001), ed. C. Carson/K. Shepard. New York/Boston: IPM/Warner Books.

Ball, Charles (1836). *Slavery in the United States: A Narrative of the Life and Adventures of Charles Ball, a Black Man.* Lewiston, PA: John W. Shugert.

Barrett, Charles Kingsley (1975). *The Gospel of John and Judaism*, tr. Dwight Moody Smith. Philadelphia: Fortress.

"B.C." Attrib. Benjamin Clark (1820). "On Seeing a Mourning Ring Inscribed with the Words, 'Not Lost, but Gone Before,'" *Evangelical Magazine.*

Bockie, Simon (1993). *Death and the Invisible Powers: The World of Kongo Belief.* Bloomington/Indianapolis: Indiana Univ.

Conyers, Richard (1772). *A Collection of Psalms and Hymns from Various Authors: For the Use of Serious and Devout Christians of All Denominations*. London: Clement Watts.

Crew, Spencer R./Bunch III, Lonnie G./Price, Clement A., eds. (2015). *Memories of the Enslaved: Voices from the Slave Narratives*. Santa Barbara/Denver: Praeger.

"Death of Mrs. Louisa Gaillard: Was Born in 1809 and Was Daughter of a Revolutionary Officer (April 5, 1902). The *State* (Columbia, SC newspaper), p. 6, col. 4.

Freud, Sigmund (1957/1915 original). "Mourning and Melancholia." *The Standard Edition of the Complete Psychological Works of Sigmund Freud*, tr. James Strachey. London: Hogarth/Institute of Psycho-Analysis, 14:243-258.

"Hamp Kennedy" (1941). Federal Writers' Project: *Slave narrative project*, vol. 9, Mississippi, Allen-Young, 84-90. Washington DC: United States Works Projects Administration Records, Manuscript Division, Library of Congress.

Hengel, Martin (1977). *Crucifixion in the Ancient World and the Folly of the Message of the Cross*, tr. John Bowden. Philadelphia: Fortress.

https://en.wikipedia.org/wiki/Dylann_Roof

https://www.goodreads.com/quotes/7139789-that-reservoir-of-goodness-beyond-and-of-another-kind-that

https://www.theguardian.com/us-news/2015/jul/10/confederate-flag-south-carolina-statehouse

https://www.viralbeliever.com/christian-quotes-about-death-afterlife/

"Jefferson Franklin Henry" (1941). Federal Writers' Project: *Slave narrative project*, vol. 4, Georgia, part 2, Garey-Jones, 178-193. Washington DC: United States Works Projects Administration Records, Manuscript Division, Library of Congress.

Kübler-Ross, Elisabeth (1964). *On Death and Dying: What the Dying Have to Teach Doctors, Nurses, Clergy, and Their Own Families*. New York/Toronto: Macmillan.

Lincoln, Abraham (November 19, 1863 manuscript). *Address Delivered at the Dedication of the Cemetery at Gettysburg*. https://gettysburg150concerts.files.wordpress.com/2012/11/gettysburg-address2.jpg

Lindemann, Erich (1944). "Symptomatology and Management of Acute Grief." *American Journal of Psychiatry*, 101/2, 141-148.

MacArthur, Douglas (April 6, 1964). "Prayer for My Son." New York *Times*, reprint: https://www.newyorktimes.com/1964/04/06/archives/macarthur-leaves-a-spiritual-legacy-prayer-for-his-son.html

Mason, Lowell/Webb, George James (1850). *Cantica Laudis or the American Book of Church Music.* New York/Boston: Mason & Law/Tappan, Whittemore, & Mason.

McDonald, Nicole Danielle (2016). *A Prophetic Witness in Pastoral Worship: Preaching Funerals for Christians Who Are Unknown to Clergy.* Unpublished D.Min. project, Louisville (KY) Presbyterian Theological Seminary.

Murray, Iain H. (1994). *Revival and Revivalism: The Making and Marring of American Evangelicalism, 1750-1858.* Edinburgh/Carlisle: Banner of Truth Trust.

Myers, Peter D. (1850). *Zion Songster: A Collection of Hymns and Spiritual Songs, Generally Sung at Camp and Prayer Meetings, and in Revivals of Religion*, 3rd ed. New York: J. S. Redfield.

"Ned Walker" (1941). Project 1655, Federal Writers' Project: *Slave narrative project*, v. 14, South Carolina, Part 4, Raines-Young, pp. 174-180. Washington DC: United States Works Projects Administration Records, Manuscript Division, Library of Congress.

Newton, John/Cowper, William (1779). *Olney Hymns in Three Books.* London: W. Oliver.

Rando, Therese (1993). *Treatment of Complicated Mourning.* Champaign, IL: Research Press.

Smith, Suzanne E. (2010). *To Serve the Living: Funeral Directors and the African American Way of Death.* Cambridge/London: Harvard Univ.

Sursum Corda (1898). Philadelphia: American Baptist Publication Society.

United States Federal Census (1870). Fairfield County, SC.

Walker, William (1854). *Southern Harmony and Musical Companion.* Philadelphia: Miller & Burlock.

Walther, Johann (1524). *Ein geystliche Gesangk Buchleyn.* Wittenberg.

Watts, Isaac (1707-1709). *Hymns and Spiritual Songs.* London: J. Hanseys (?).

Wherry, Peter M. (2013). *Preaching Funerals in the Black Church: Bringing Perspective to Pain.* Valley Forge: Judson.

White, Benjamin Franklin/King, Elisha J. (1844). *The sacred harp: A collection of psalm and hymn tunes, odes, and anthems, selected from the most eminent authors.* Philadelphia: T. K. & P. G. Collins, 1844.

Painted windows in the fellowship hall of Highland Baptist Church, Louisville, KY: Above: Sixteenth Street Baptist Church bombing victims Denise McNair, Carole Robertson, Addie Mae Collins, and Cynthia Wesley. Below: Martin Luther King, Jr.

Early Sources

CHRISTIAN SCRIPTURE

1 Corinthians
1:23   54
2:9   77
3:10   40
11:17-26   95
15   33
15:12-20   34
15:20-26   57-58
15:54   62
15:55   76

2 Corinthians
5:1   78
5:8   51

2 Timothy
4:6-7   76

Acts
16:23-26   138-140

Hebrews
12:1   44, 156
11:13   116

John
1:1-4   60-61
3:16   101
6:30-51   95
8:32   59
10:30   60
12:32   61
19:30   54

Luke
13:1-5   37

Luke (cont'd)		*1 Samuel (cont'd)*	
15:11-32	35-36	16:18	73
22:14-20	97-99, 103	17:45-47	73
22:15	100		
22:16-18	95	*Deuteronomy*	
22:19	102	21:23	54
22:20	101		
23:43	139	*Ecclesiastes*	
		3:1-2	51
Mark			
4:39	105, 108	*Genesis*	
14:1-25	96	3:19	45
14:24	96		
		Isaiah	
Philippians		2:4	156
1:6	63	11:6	91
		53:3	47
Revelation (Apocalypse)			
13	91	*Job*	
21:4	77	23:10	63
21:23	77		
		Numbers	
Romans		23:19	61
5:1-5	116, 123		
6:9	57	*Proverbs*	
8:28	52	4:7	59
		Psalms	
JEWISH SCRIPTURE		1	49
		16:11	52
1 Chronicles		23	19
12:8	69-70, 74	24:1	57
1 Samuel			
16:7	73		

NON-CANONICAL LITERATURE

Didache
9-10   95

Tractate Semahot
2:11   54

A stained glass given by residents of Wales to Sixteenth Street Baptist Church, Birmingham, AL commemorates the 1963 bombing that killed four children at that church. The window also brings to mind Robert Hassell's meditation on Jesus' Crucifixion and its aftermath as a source of hope following a tragic death. (Courtesy National Geographic Image Collection / Alamy Stock Photo.)

General Index

Aiken, James	137	Boston Celtics	40
Aiken, Louisa Gaillard	137	Boston Univ.	79
Aiken, Pompey	137-138	*Brethren, we*	16, 20,
Ali, Muhammad	155	*have met*	139
Allen, Elmer Lucille	155	Brice, Walt	9, 148
Amazing Grace		*Broad is the road*	
(see *Faith's Review*)		(see *The Almost Xn*)	
And am I born to die	11	Burke, George	31
Anderson, Marian	82	Burke, Shirley	31
Apple Corporation	68	Charleston, SC	7
BaKongo customs	5, 10, 22-23	Christ Temple Xn Life Ctr.	46
Ball, Charles	6, 7, 13	Civil Rights Act	87
Barrett, Charles K.	96	Civilian Conser-	131
Bates, Daisy	90	vation Corps	
Beecher, Lyman	15	Clark, Benjamin	154
Bennett III, Winston G.	29, 31	Clay Jr., Cassius	
Bennett Jr., Winston G.	39-42	(see Ali, Muhammad)	
Bethel AME Zion Ch.	9, 136	Cleveland Cavs	40
Bethune, Mary	90	Clifton Place	133, 142-143. 146
Billups Sr., Charlie F.	104		
Birmingham, AL	80-87		

Cockerham, H. D.	66-67	Emanuel AME Church	112-115
Codex Vaticanus	96		
Cognitive dissonance	30, 81	Emotional expression	14-15, 20-21
Coke Memorial UMC	48		
Cole, Robert A.	10	Epideictic speech	31
Coleman-Singleton, Sharonda	120, 129		
		Evers, Medgar	84, 89
Collins, Addie Mae	162	Fairfield Co., SC	132, 136
Concord Presbyt. Ch.	9	*Faith's Review & Expectation*	122-123, 128-129
Confederate flag	123-124		
Consolatio genre	32	Faulkner, Wm.	135
Constitution, U.S.	114	Federal Writers' Project	29, 131
Consumption (see Tuberculosis)			
		Fewell, Bessie (nee Walker)	147
Corpse bathing	13		
Corte de Culebra (see Culebra Cut)		First Baptist Ch. Charleston, SC	14
Cowper, William	123, 149	Flags	3, 10
Crozer Theological Seminary	34, 79	Flowers	3, 10
		Freud, Sigmund	23-24
Culebra Cut	144	Funeral processions	2-3, 13, 19-20
David (Judahite king)	72		
Davis, Jefferson	147	Gaillard Cut (see Culebra Cut)	
Deductive reasoning	33		
Deep River	8	Gaillard quarters	145-146
Dialectical reasoning	33-34	Gaillard, Alfred	143
Dixon, William W.	132	Gaillard, David DuBose	143-144
Dwight, Elizabeth P.	142		
Dwight, Maria L.	143	Gaillard, David St. Pierre	133, 142
Ellis, James A. (Jimmy)	155		
Ellison, Bob	143	Gaillard Henry	134, 137-138, 144, 145
Ellison, David	143		
Ellison, DuBose	143		
Ellison, Katharine L.	143	Gaillard, Louisa	25-27, 133, 142
Emancipation Proc.	81, 133		

General Index

Gaillard, Richard	143	Kentuckians for the Cmwth.	154
Gaillard, Samuel	143		
Gazaway, Marshall	155	King Jr., Martin Luther	29, 32-34, 79-87, 115, 121, 162
Goliath (Philistine)	73		
Great Depression	131		
Gullah/Geechee culture	6		
Hamlet	83-84, 92		
Hampton, Wade	143	King, Coretta S.	115
Hark from the tombs	11	Kübler-Ross, Elisabeth	24, 66
Hassell, Robert O.	32		
Heath, Leander	140	Lance, Ethel	120, 129
Heath, Nora	55, 147	Lincoln Mem.	82
Hengel, Martin	55	Lincoln, Abraham	147, 156
Henry, Jefferson F.	12		
Henry, Pompey	137	Lindemann, Erich	24
Hurd, Cynthia	120, 128		
Hyde, Ruby	155	Luther, Martin	8
I have a dream	32, 81-85	Lydia (slave)	7
Inductive reasoning	33-35	MacArthur, Douglas	67
Islamic practice	13, 30		
Jackson, Mahalia	90	Martin, Robert	68
Jackson, Susie	120, 129	McDonald, Nicole D.	29, 31, 36
James, Carla	44		
Jeffersonville (IN) High School	42	McNair, Denise	162
		Middleton-Doctor, DePayne	120, 129
Jim Crow laws	121, 124		
Johnson, Sam	146	Miller, Zephra	155
Joiner, Gemayel	67	*Mit Fried und Freud*	8
Joiner, Gerald J.	31		
Joiner, Jon'a F.	67	Moncks Corner, SC	142
Joiner, Luevern	70, 72		
Joiner, Taurean Delon	65-78	Moore, Wash	135, 148-149
Joiner, Zoe	67		
Judaism	30	Moore, William	84, 89-90
Kennedy, Hamp	12		

Morehouse College	79	Poor people's march on DC	81, 85-86
Mpemba	22	Prayer of Douglas Macarthur	71-72
My country, 'tis of thee	82	Proctor, Samuel	34
National Basketball Assoc.	40	*Promised Land*	8
Nettleton, Asahel	15	Psychoanalytic theory	22-23
New England Revivals	15	Rando, Therese	28
Newton, John	123	rev.com	40
Nobel Peace Prize	87	Riley Jr., Joseph	122
Norton Cancer Center	68	Robertson, Carole	162
Nurses (female attendants)	18-20	Robinson, Marilyn	128
O little town of Bethlehem	17-18	Roof, Dylan	112-113
Obama, Barack	29-31, 111-114	Roosevelt, Franklin D.	131, 147
Oh freedom	8, 13	*Sacred Harp*	11
On seeing a mourning ring	154	Samuel (prophet)	72
Owens, Joseph	67	Sanders, Twanza	120, 129
Passover	96-100	Sandy Creek Baptist Ch. (NC)	14
Paul	33	Saul (Judahite king)	72
Pentecostal Movements	15	Second Great Awakening	4, 14
Pinckney, Clementa	112, 115 117-129	*See how the scriptures are fulfilling*	16-17
Pompey (preacher)	31, 34-35, 148-149	Shuttlesworth, Fred	86
		Simmons, Daniel	120, 129

GENERAL INDEX

Sixteenth Street Baptist Ch. 32, 80-81, 86, 88, 90
Smoketown Neighborhood Assoc. 154
Social Security Act 135
Soon I will be done with the troubles of the world 8
Southern Christian Leadership Conf. 86
Southern Harmony 11
Spring Vale plantation 133, 136
Springvale AME Ch. 136, 146-148
Spurgeon, Charles 56
St. John Epis. Ch. 136-137, 142
Stennett, Samuel 8
Stone, Dave 68
Taylor, Troy 40
The Almost Christian 155
Theodicy 32-33, 82
There is a balm in Gilead 156
There is a fountain filled with blood 149
There is a land of pure Delight 8
Thirteenth amendment 134
Thompson, Myra 120, 129
Traumatic loss 53-54
Tuberculosis 7, 148
Turner, Nat 115
Unity Monument 154
University of Kentucky 40
University of Louisville 41
Unknown decedent 36-37
Veal, Pompey 137
Vesey, Denmark 114
Vesey, Robert 115
Vietnam War 87
Voting Rights Act 87
Walker, Sylvia (nee Field) 147
Walker, Bess (Ned's mother) 145
Walker, Clerissie 145
Walker, June 145
Walker, Ned 9, 25-27, 132-141
Walker, Phibbie 145
Walker, Renah 145
Walker, Susana (alt. Susannah) 147
Walker, Tom 144
Wateree Creek 134, 142
Watts, Isaac 8, 11
Wesley, Charles 11-12
Wesley, Cynthia 162
Wherry, Peter M. 34
White Oak, SC 140
Why do we mourn departing friends? 11
Winnsboro, SC 140-141, 144
Winnsboro Mill, SC 141
Works Progress Administration 131
Zion Baptist Church, Inc. 64

www.ingramcontent.com/pod-product-compliance
Lightning Source LLC
Chambersburg PA
CBHW022011160426
43197CB00007B/376